THE BIBLE:

How To Read, Understand, And Study The Bible

D1409116

Bible Notes for Beginners
Bible University Press

TABLE OF CONTENTS

INTRODUCTION

Welcome To Bible Notes for Beginners

The Bible is an incredible book. When we are discouraged it can offer us hope, when we're afraid it can help us feel reassured, and when we're excited and brimming over with joy, it has the ability to perfectly capture what we want to say.

Yet sometimes it can also be confusing. If we're honest, we don't always know how to read certain passages. For example, when Jesus says: "If I, therefore, the master and teacher, have washed your feet, you ought to wash one another's feet. I have given you a model to follow, so that as I have done for you, you should also do" (John 13:14-15), does this mean that we should actually wash one another's feet or that we should behave humbly with each other? Maybe at church we should have foot-washings, alongside of Bible study and evangelism classes?

What about other passages like those that command not tattooing our skin (Leviticus 19:28), or Paul's statement about hair styles: "does not nature itself teach you that if a man wears his hair long it is a disgrace to him, whereas if a woman has long hair it is her glory, because long hair has been given [her] for a covering" (1 Corinthians 11:14-15)? Are Christians with tattoos in sin? Are women with short hair disgraced? Are men with long hair behaving disgracefully in God's eyes? Before we say that was just the custom at the time, note that Paul grounds his argument *in nature, not custom* ("does not *nature itself teach you* …").

These are just some of the types of questions that can come up when we are trying to understand God's word. This would all be fine if we were just studying it for curiosity's sake, but chances are if you're reading this book, you also want to live it out. Whether you're a believer whose either grown up in a Christian home and come to realize how true it is, or you've recently put your faith in Jesus, and want to follow him, this is important to you. The reason is because when we love someone we want to do right by them. It is no different with our Lord. This is why the better we can understand the Scriptures, the better we will understand him, and the better we will be able to align our lives with what makes him happy.

Bible Notes is a series intended to help us learn how to better read and understand the Bible. This book gives a broad overview to the entire Bible: explaining its different genres so that we can read it, interpret it, and study it. Other books in the Bible Notes Series will go deeper, focusing on specific books in the Bible, and giving us more information about their unique way of talking and thinking about God. If you are serious student of God's Word, this is the series for you!

I promise you if you commit yourself to learning the Bible, you'll be blessed. This isn't just my word though, it's also God's:

> *Blessed is the man who does not walk*
> *in the counsel of the wicked,*
> *Nor stand in the way of sinners,*
> *nor sit in company with scoffers.*
> **2**
> *Rather, the law of the Lord is his joy;*
> *and on his law he meditates day and night.*
> **3**
> *He is like a tree*
> *planted near streams of water,*
> *that yields its fruit in season;*
> *Its leaves never wither;*
> *whatever he does prospers.*

Psalms 1:1-3

CHAPTER 1

Our Approach To Studying The Bible

Biblical Theology

When we first approach the Bible we need to realize that it isn't simply a book, *but a collection of several different books*. There are sixty-six books in all, and a different human author has written each of them.

While as Christians we believe that God has inspired each human writer to write their books, we also believe that the human authors contributed. The idea that God helped them write their book is called "inspiration" and there have been lots of different ways in which Christians throughout history have understood how God has helped them write their books. Here are two biblical passages where this idea is mentioned:

16 All scripture is inspired by God and is useful for teaching, for refutation, for correction, and for training in righteousness, 17 so that one who belongs to God may be competent, equipped for every good work. 2 Timothy 3:16-17

21 for no prophecy ever came through human will; but rather human beings moved by the Holy Spirit spoke under the influence of God. 2 Peter 1:21

Both verses tell us (1) that human beings were moved by the Holy Spirit and spoke under God's influence, and that (2) this quality applies to *all* scripture. This means the entire Bible is inspired and ultimately written by God.

But Christians throughout history have also believed that God didn't simply override the human authors, but used them. This is called a "confluence" theory of inspiration, and it's why different books have different styles to them. Some writers like to use the same kinds of words or phrases, some think about God in one way, while others a slightly different way. This doesn't mean they contradict each other (remember, they're all inspired), but that they each have their own styles, and that God used those different styles to communicate to all of us. We are all a little different from each other and God has chosen different people to communicate to all types of us. You may find as you get to know certain writers' styles that you're drawn to one over another. That's okay. They're all inspired, but one may just say it more in a way that you relate to.

This will be important because as we begin to learn more we will be able to talk about each writer's unique style. Biblical scholars refer to this unique style or way of talking about God as *biblical theology*. While systematic theology tries to systematize or take what *the entire Bible* teaches on a topic, biblical theology tries to understand how *each writer* chose to say or think about things.

Genres

Additionally, each of the Bible's different books contains different types of literature. People who read literature and study the Bible a lot refer to these different types of books as *genres*. So, for example, poetry is one type of genre, or type of literature, while a proverb is another. Each type of literature is read a little differently.

Poetry for example is supposed to be read slowly. Poets like to use language to communicate an emotion, a feeling, or an idea. To do this, they often use symbolic language like a metaphor or a simile (don't worry, if you don't know what those are, we will explain it more when we get there). Take for example the Psalm I quoted in the Introduction. The writer compares the person who reads God's word to a tree that is planted by a stream of water who's leaves fully grow (Ps 1:3). Does this mean that we are literally trees? Of course not! Instead it is an analogy.

Israel is a dry place that relies on rain for water. When it doesn't rain, things get dry, and things like trees and plants dry up. When the rains come, the water gets trapped in natural rock reservoirs called *Wadi*. The poet is here saying that the person who reads God's word will be like one of those trees that's lucky enough to drink up water from the wadi after a large rain storm. It'll grow, have beautiful leaves, while all the other trees that aren't so lucky will dry up. So there's a contrast: all sorts of dried up trees and one growing beautifully with lots of leaves. The poet is using this image to say that's exactly what it feels like to be in God's word all the time: everyone around you is dry and bitter, while you have a source of nourishment.

Different genres have different rules. These rules aren't arbitrary, they're just how that type of literature "works." So, for example, a movie is different than a comic strip. A poem is different than a proverb. This means that things often mean one thing in a certain kind of genre and something different in another. For example, if you were reading something and it said: "the Kings kill the ducks," this would mean one thing if it was the front page of a newspaper, and another if it was in the sports section of the same newspaper. In the first example, you'd probably wonder how loud those pesky ducks were quacking to make those murderous kings kill them, while in the other you'd know they aren't actually Kings or Ducks, but hockey teams.

It's the same thing when we read the Bible. Some books are stories or narratives, which are kind of like movies today. They have a beginning, middle, and an end. The way a storyteller tells you something is by repeating an idea over and over again throughout their story, or by having certain images get repeated again and again. If you were to pick the story up in the middle, it is likely that you could misunderstand what it going on. Just think of how you feel when you walk in on a movie halfway through, or leave to use the restroom then come back and realize you missed a really important part of the story. Likewise, if we were to pick up books in the Bible that are stories and begin in the middle or end, we are likely to misread it or get totally confused. This doesn't mean you aren't smart, it just means you're reading it wrong.

However, in a letter the writer can be a lot more direct. They will often just tell you what they are thinking. The challenge with a letter is that often it is written to someone else and we only have only one half of the conversation. This is kind of what it is like when we are reading Paul's letters to the Romans or the Corinthians. In the Corinthian letters for example, we know they had already written Paul and Paul is trying to answer some of their questions (1 Corinthians 7:1), but what exactly did the letter say? We just don't know. When we read a letter, therefore, we want to be aware we are entering into someone else's conversation. We will talk more about this later.

This Book's Approach: Genre

As we approach our study of the Bible, we want to keep both of these things in mind: first, the Bible is collection of different books. This means we will want to learn how different writers talk and express things. Second, the Bible is written in different genres or types of literature.

As mentioned in the Introduction, Bible Notes is part of a series. Of the things we just mentioned: biblical theology and genre, this book will deal primarily with genre. My goal is to help you get a sense of how to pay attention to the different types of literature within the Bible. Other Bible Note books will delve more into how each biblical writer thinks about God and how he is working in history (i.e., biblical theology). Both are essential to really learning how to read the Bible. So for example, while this book is providing a broad introduction to biblical genres like "Old Testament Narratives," I cannot get into the specifics of a book like Genesis since this book is meant to be an introduction and survey. A future book in the Bible Notes Series, however, entitled "How to Read Genesis," will give more detail about Genesis' sub genres, and its biblical theology.

You'll want to start with this book and then pick up the volumes that touch on the specific biblical book you are most interested in learning.

One Final Thing And A Word Of Encouragement

Translations

As we begin our study of the Bible, we want to be aware that we are reading a translation from the original languages it was written in. No need to worry, though. There are a lot of great English translations! I'm not just saying this either. I used to teach students how to read the original Greek and even learned how to also read the Bible in the original Hebrew and Aramaic (and some Syriac for good measure!), and I realized something pretty obvious: It said basically the same thing! Yes, there were little things here and there that made it more insightful, but most of the time it was simply saying the same thing I could read in my English translation. In fact, most translations are done by groups of scholars who are very good with the original languages and have done an excellent job.

The only thing I would suggest is finding one that is a little more literal. Some translations try to make it more readable, while others keep it closer to the original. Some literal translations are the New American Standard Bible (NASB), or the Revised Standard Bible (RSV). The New International Version is somewhere in-between. It stays close to the original language, but sometimes tries to create the "dynamic equivalent" to what it would be in English. I personally really enjoy it, but find the translation that is best for you.

A Word of Encouragement

As you begin to become sensitive to things like genre, biblical theology, and some helpful study skills you'll begin to develop your own idea of what certain passages or books *mean*. This is the best part because you'll begin to feel empowered. When you go to church you can be thoughtful. You may sit there and think, "wow, this guy really understands it well! I'm so moved!" Or sometimes, you may realize even the pastor doesn't understand it quite as well as you thought. I don't mean this to be arrogant, I just mean as you begin to make connections you'll also begin to see when others around you are making connections too. Again, you may realize people you thought knew the Bible really well maybe don't understand it as well as you thought. Sometimes, that can be a little disheartening, but at least you can be thoughtful and not have to just rely on what someone tells you, but trust your own ability to read and understand God's word. Remember: God loves you very much and he's made you in his image, which means he believes you're capable and worthy to understand it ... that's why he gave it to you in the first place! Trust God's work in your life, learn some of these basic skills, and I promise you the Bible will become a very different book, and you'll become a very different person. With that, let's begin.

CHAPTER 2

Old Testament Narratives: Learn To Watch The Movie

Perhaps the best place for us to start is with what makes up the majority of the Bible. The Old Testament makes up three-quarters of the entire Bible, and of that, 40% of the Old Testament is a genre known as *narrative*. In fact the following books are almost entirely narrative: Genesis, Joshua, Judges, Ruth, 1 and 2 Samuel, 1 and 2 Kings, 1 and 2 Chronicles, Ezra, Nehemiah, Daniel, Jonah, and Haggai. In addition, Exodus, Numbers, Jeremiah, Ezekiel, Isaiah, and Job contain large portions of narrative. Finally, the Gospels and Acts in the New Testament are also predominantly narrative.

This means that if you devote yourself to learning some basic skills in reading narratives, you will be well on your way to becoming an informed reader of close to half of the Bible! Not bad.

Watching The Movie

Narratives are essentially, stories. By story we simply mean something that has a beginning, middle, and end. A good story often has *characters*, which are the people within the story, and a *plot,* which is what the story is about: typically in every story there is a problem that needs to be resolved and the main character will be the hero who solves it after going through some sort of trial he or she needs to overcome. Finally, a story will have a *setting*, which is where or when the story occurs.

I titled this chapter "learning to watch the movie," because in our culture we often don't read many works of fiction anymore, but we do often go to the movies. Movies are narratives. Let's take a popular movie as one example.

Star Wars is perhaps one of the most iconic films of the last thirty years, so it is a great example. It's likely that even if you haven't ever seen the movie, you still have a rough idea of what it is about. As a Star Wars purist, I'm going to be a little snobbish and only refer to the original films: Star Wars, the Empire Strikes Back, and Return of the Jedi.

When the movie first begins we have the well-known "opening crawl," which tells us the events occurred "in a galaxy far, far away ..." This is the *setting*. Before we see or hear anything, we are told that the story we are about to watch occurred in the distant past and in a distant galaxy within space. The details in the crawl give us specifics: the galaxy is undergoing a civil war with some resisting the rise an evil Empire.

As the story progresses we begin to become introduced to a cast of *characters*: Princess Leia, Darth Vader, C3PO, R2D2, and others. As the story continues we end up on an isolated planet with a young kid named Luke Skywalker who craves adventure and to make something of his life. We begin to get hints that this kid may have more to him than we at first anticipated: a fleeting conversation between his adoptive uncle and aunt implies that his father suffered a shameful demise no one wants to talk about, and this is the reason his uncle is reluctant to let him leave his farm. Apparently, no one wants him to end up like his father.

It is about this time that the *plot* is introduced. The two droids we first met have design plans to something called the Death Star. If they can give these plans to the rebels, the rebels will gain a strategic upper hand. The Empire is therefore searching for them to stop them from passing these plans along. In what looks like happenstance, Luke's uncle buys these droids. One of them insists that he belongs to someone named Obi Wan Kenobi, whom Luke wonders is a man named "Old Ben," a bizarre hermit who lives out in the desert.

Not to get into the entire story, but once Luke and "Old Ben" Kenobi meet, Luke is called on a journey: Obi Wan explains to him that his father was once a brilliant military leader and part of the defenders of the Old Republic known as the Jedi. He gives Luke his father's "light saber," a laser sword, which is really important. In all stories the hero has a crisis moment or commission: he is called to something greater, but he often believes he is not up to the task. Why in the world would anyone think *he* is able to do *this*? This is Luke's call, and he predictably shrugs it off and declines.

It isn't until his aunt and uncle are murdered that he tells Ben he wants to become a Jedi like his father. This is the beginning of the hero's journey. The rest of the movie (and sequels) hashes this out for us and we begin to realize that these two story lines are actually one: what is happening with the rebellion in their war against the Empire and Luke's journey to become a Jedi knight are connected. While the rebellion is fighting a military battle, we learn that there is a deeper spiritual war occurring between two competing forces that both can channel an unseen power known as "the Force." Darth Vader is really Luke's father, who was seduced and betrayed into following the dark side by the evil Emperor and that Princess Leia is his twin sister. Luke and Leia were separated from each and hidden from their father to protect them and in hopes that they can someday train to use the Force to save the galaxy. Luke must resist the temptation to become his father and embrace the light side. It is only once Luke can do this that the galaxy will find peace.

Biblical stories are not much different from this. Of course, the stories in the Bible are different in that they are true, but the writers want us to get caught up in the grand story that they're telling. In fact, most of the great stories that you've watched in movies are really just copies of the one that's already in the Bible (Star Wars included!).

We will get more into the details in a moment, but narratives are meant to be exciting and they sweep us up into the experience their describing. This is likely why the majority of the Bible is written in narratives … it is meant to be exciting! As we watch the movie, we get taken to another world and by identifying with the characters we vicariously experience their experiences. We may cry, we may laugh, we may feel danger all while sitting comfortably in our sits at the movie theater with a bucket of popcorn.

How To Watch The Biblical "Movie"

So how does the Bible tell us its story? First, as Fee and Stuart so artfully explain in their book <u>How To Read The Bible For All Its Worth</u>, we need to realize that there are *three levels* to biblical narratives.

Top-Level
At the "top level" is the story that is tying all of them together. It is the single "plot" that runs from Genesis through the entire Bible, and it is the grand story God wants you to understand and get excited about, and this is *his story*.

Biblical scholars refer to this story as "salvation-history" or "redemptive-history" and the *main character is God*. The plot is the story of how God gets involved in real life events and people to redeem the world. Let me explain a little more.

When we first begin reading Genesis we have the creation of the world in 1.1-2.4. This is really a poem that gives us the "big picture" of how creation was done, and tells us some very important information about the Creator. Read is carefully and you will notice a few things. First, God the Creator creates by speaking. This shows us his power. He speaks and things come into being. Second, notice all the organizing that is going on. God creates, then puts things in their proper place: birds and flying things in the air, light from darkness, etc. This is in contrast to the opening setting of the poem:

In the beginning, when God created the heavens and the earth— 2 [b] and the earth was without form or shape, with darkness over the abyss and a mighty wind sweeping over the waters—

In other words, God is taking this dark, chaotic, and unshapely world and making it orderly.

Next, the poet repeats again and again "and God saw that it was *good*" (1.4, 10, 12, 18, 21, 25, 31). When something gets repeated that much in such a short space, pay attention! What is the writer telling us? That God the Creator has benign intentions. This all-powerful God who can speak and subdue chaos, uses his power to bring about what is "good" for the world and humankind.

After the poem closes, it now switches to narrative. Beginning in 2:4 we zero in on the details of what we learned in the poem. Instead of God simply speaking, though, he is now described like a potter who forms man from the dust and breathes life into him. This is an intimate picture. God is not just powerful, but nurturing. There is also a garden in the east in Eden (*setting!*) where God places humankind. Here he plants delightful looking trees, which are good for food and in the middle of the garden a tree of life and the tree of the knowledge of good and evil. God commands man:

You are free to eat from any of the trees of the garden 17 except the tree of knowledge of good and evil. From that tree you shall not eat; when you eat from it you shall die.

The perceptive reader should immediately make a connection: the tree which man is not allowed to eat is the very thing the poet just told us God is concerned about: "the good." In other words, humankind cannot take the knowledge of good and evil into their own hands, but need to trust that the benevolent Creator knows what is "the good" for them and for his world.

It is this very thing that the serpent tempts the woman with. Note again the language:

But the snake said to the woman: "You certainly will not die! 5 God knows well that when you eat of it your eyes will be opened and you will be like gods, who know good and evil." *6* The woman saw that the tree was good *for food and pleasing to the eyes, and the tree was desirable for gaining wisdom. So she took some of its fruit and ate it; and she also gave some to her husband, who was with her, and he ate it. 7 Then the eyes of both of them were opened, and they knew that they were naked; so they sewed fig leaves together and made loincloths for themselves.*

Two things: the serpent makes it clear that to know what is "good" is the rightful prerogative of the gods, not humankind, but adds that the Creator's command is not well-intentioned. In other words, he doesn't want what's good, he is trying to keep something good from you! Second, the woman then looks and sees that the tree is "good" and wants it for herself and her husband.

At this point the created order is thrown into chaos again: the creature has rebelled against the Creator and the result is that humankind is banished from life (3:22a) and cursed to live in exile (3:22b). What follows from chapter four to eleven is a vicious cycle: chapter four shows us that rather than brotherhood humankind has become selfish, even murderous. Chapter five gives us the genealogy of Adam, which is really about fast-forwarding the movie to get us to another important moment: namely, that humankind has proliferated and God regrets making them (chapter six). This is so bad, that God intends to "un-create" the world – i.e., he will again bring the great deep, that covered the earth in 1:2, over the earth to wipe out all life (7:11-12). There is one man, however, that is just so God will use him to start over (6:5-13).

Regretfully, the story ends badly. Shortly after the flood Noah becomes just like Adam. Just as Adam, the person responsible to till the ground in the garden of Eden ate the from the tree through his wife, so Noah "a man of the soil" drinks from the "fruit of the vine" and also uncovers his nakedness (9:20-24). Noah's descendants also become wicked and try to usurp God's role by building a tower to heaven (11:1-9).

This is where the story slows way down and God calls Abram from Ur of the Chaldeans (12:1-3):

The Lord had said to Abram, "Go from your country, your people and your father's household to the land I will show you.

"I will make you into a great nation,
    and I will bless you;
I will make your name great,
    and you will be a blessing.

I will bless those who bless you,
    and whoever curses you I will curse;
and all peoples on earth
    will be blessed through you."

This begins the "grand story" of the entire rest of the Bible and lays out the essential *plot* that God will be working out: he will call a single person, Abram, whom he will later rename Abraham, and make his family into a nation, this nation will eventually restore blessing to "all the peoples of the earth."

This is what the entire rest of the Bible is all about. I like to say that it is from this point on that we will see God painstakingly and very patiently get his hands dirty. This grand story isn't going to be accomplished by grand sweeping acts, but through day-to-day things, like helping a rejected and insecure woman finally have a child for the first time (chapters 16-17, 21), using the jealousy and cruelty of brothers to ultimately bless and protect the same family who betrayed their loyalty (37:12-50). In fact, he will use the very act of their cruel jealousy to pave the way for them to go to Egypt so they can be protected during famine, and there grow them from one family of seventy people to a nation with children as numerous as the sand (Exodus 1:1-7) – just like he here promised Abraham. Again and again, God steps onto the scene: when he calls Moses to lead them out of Egypt, when he raises up King David, and so on - all to accomplish these simple words to Abraham; and he is doing it to ultimately "bless all peoples."

Paul even goes so far as to say that these promises to Abraham are actually the Gospel (Galatians 3:8). You probably thought the Gospel was just the death and resurrection of Jesus, but not for Paul. For Paul it meant quite a bit more. We don't have time to discuss it here, but in a later book I'll explain this. Remember, Paul is the "Apostle to the Gentiles" – so that is a big hint!

My point is that the top-level of the Bible's narratives are *about God, not people.* He is the main character and all the people in the story are the way in which he is working in history to accomplish his plan of bringing blessing to the nations. While Genesis 1-11 covers a period of about 2,000 years, Genesis 12-50 covers only a period of about 200. We know this because we can add up the dates in the genealogies to help give us an idea. The point is that the writer has used chapters 1-11 to set up the context, and he really wants us to read the rest as God's story. That story is the whole point!

Middle-Level
The middle-level to Biblical narratives are about Israel. Remember, God promised Abraham that he would make him into a great nation (12:2). This means that the stories about Abraham, Isaac, Jacob, Joseph, Moses, and more are explaining to us how he is creating that nation.

Bottom-Level
The bottom-level of biblical narratives are the individual stories, which can change characters or settings. So, for example, we can talk about the Abraham stories, or the Joseph Cycle. Each of these are self-contained stories with their own beginning, middle, and end.

The crucial thing to recognize is that these smaller stories are really the story of Israel, which is really the story of salvation-history. We cannot read the individual stories and lose sight of this bigger picture.

Conclusion
So what can we draw from this?

First, the Old Testament stories are not just stories about people who lived in Old Testament times. They are first and foremost, stories about God and how God was working in their lives to accomplish his larger plan. *God is the hero of these stories, not the human characters.* In other words, while Abraham or Joseph may be a main character, the true main character is behind the scenes orchestrating the events to accomplish His plan.

Second, theses stories are not abstracted and allegorized stories of how God works in each of our lives. Let me explain because I know how that can sound. Remember, these stories are about *how God is working in history to save the world* this means that Abraham was unique. Moses was unique. Sarah was unique. God worked in their lives at a specific moment in history to accomplish a specific thing. He was painstakingly building towards his plan. You and I live at a different moment in that plan. If you are reading this, chances are that you are not Jewish or a part of the nation of Israel: this means you are one of the "nations" i.e., non-Jews he wanted to bless, and guess what? You're receiving at least part of that blessing right now! We cannot take a historical moment and use that as an allegory about all people in all places.

Now, the writer may intend to teach us lessons from their lives. This is different, and we will have clues to that in the story itself. Just as Luke Skywalker can teach us something when we watch Star Wars, but we would never leave the theater and think that we are actually Luke Skywalker! That is unless you want to be committed. In the same way, the biblical writers will use their characters to teach us lessons, but they will give us clues of what those lessons are and we cannot confuse this and conflate ourselves with those characters. Abraham was a real person who existed in history and what God did in and through him he did to create what is here now. It isn't going to happen again and he isn't doing that with you now. I hate to break it to you, but he didn't give you the promise of Genesis 1-3 to make you into a great nation, as much as you may like that.

Third, biblical stories do not teach us directly, but indirectly. Again, let me explain. When we read something like a letter, the writer comes right out and tells us something. Maybe it is that they want you to start behaving a certain way or that they hope to see you soon. In a story, the storyteller wants you to infer what the point is. For example, when we watch a movie, the director rarely comes up and speaks directly to you, instead they tell a story and it is up to you to infer what the movie was about.

How do storytellers give you clues? First, they will often repeat things. You may hear a key phrase or sentence get repeated. You may have images that keep re-appearing. Within Star Wars there are lots of these: the idea of the Force, the idea of faith in adversity, the idea of a small band of rebels defeating a great, evil Empire. All of these ideas tell us that the storyteller wants us to go away and think about the use and misuse of power, what it means for something to be unified, and how change happens. It isn't through aggression, but through patient struggle, and that even the "little guy" can turn out to be an all-powerful Jedi. Ironically, it also means that even the "big bad guy" can turn out to be a lonely, mangled man who is ultimately saved by the love of his son.

Second, these clues are given *throughout the whole story*. Stories demand we treat them like wholes. When we walk in on a movie that is halfway through we often end up confused, and when we just watch a single scene in a movie without watching the rest we are bound to misunderstand what's important. It is exactly the same with biblical narratives. When we pick up the Bible and beginning reading Genesis in chapter twenty, you are essentially starting a movie that is halfway through. No wonder it can feel so confusing! We need to learn to read it as a whole. This means reading it from the beginning, then coming back and continuing it later, but while remembering what you were reading the day before. Learn to track the plot as it is moving. It will make much more sense.

Learn to have an eye for some of these things and begin to appreciate the grand movie God wants you to see. I mentioned earlier that you are not the characters and that is true in the sense I explained it – but there is something else. *You are a character in a different sense.* God is still unfolding his plan today (albeit differently than he did with Abraham or Moses) and he wants you to realize that. As much as he patiently worked with Sarah, he is still patiently working with you. Will you help him bring blessing to the nations?

CHAPTER 3

The Law: Guidelines For Living In A Contract

After narratives, perhaps the next major portion of the Old Testament is the Law. In fact, the traditional Jewish way of organizing how the books within the Hebrew Bible are grouped, is within three broad categories: the Law, the Prophets, and the Writings (See, Luke 24:44).

But what is the Law? This can be a little confusing since the Bible uses the term to refer to a few different things. First, the Bible will often refer to the first five books of the Old Testament as "the Law." This includes all of these books even those sections of them that do not actually contain legal material. So, for example, Joshua 1:8 says the following:

Do not let this book of the law depart from your lips. Recite it by day and by night, that you may carefully observe all that is written in it; then you will attain your goal; then you will succeed.

Here, Joshua was instructed to read that book, which Moses had written, namely, the material from Genesis to Deuteronomy.

Secondly, sometimes New Testament writers will use the phrase to refer to the entire Old Testament (Matthew 5:17-19; Luke 16:17; Titus 3:9). This is probably the case because even though the Prophets and Writings do not include "the Law," their intent is related to it somehow. We will actually get more into this in our chapter on the Prophets because it is crucial to properly understand how to read them.

Lastly, "the Law" very specifically refers to that large body of legal material, which begins at Exodus 20 and continues through the end of Deuteronomy. When we look at this large body of material we will see that the vast majority of it concerns legal issues: the ritual purity of certain types of food, keeping the Sabbath day, and much more.

These passages raise a lot of questions for modern Christians. Namely, how are we to relate to this material? Let's briefly discuss this before giving you some helpful pointers on how to read legal material.

The Law is a Contract
When we first approach the concept of "the Law," we need to remember that the Law is situated within the covenant God entered into with the people of Israel through Moses. A covenant is a binding contract between two parties, both of whom typically having obligations within the agreement. I will come back to this, but let me briefly explain what a covenant in Old Testament times was all about.

Within Old Testament times there were different types of covenants that people typically entered into. Typically there was an all-powerful suzerain, who oversaw a weaker, dependent vassal. The powerful suzerain would promise to protect and do certain things for this weaker party so long as the weaker party likewise agreed to do certain things for the suzerain. If the weaker vassal kept to the agreement he could be assured that the suzerain would protect him and follow through on his commitments. If the vassal failed to do what the suzerain commanded however, then there was no obligation for the suzerain to act on his or her behalf.

Within this framework adhering to the suzzerain's obligations were considered loyalty or righteousness, because you had made a promise to do certain things. Following through on that proved you were loyal, a just or righteous person who could be depended on, and truthful – in the sense of not being dishonest or misleading with your promises. Likewise, a vassal can all upon a suzerain to be righteous, which meant essentially, "show me you are also trust-worthy and are willing to keep the commitments you entered into in our agreement." Likewise, the suzerain could be called "true," "honest," etc.

It is the same type of thing we do all the time. If I enter into an agreement with someone, both of us are committing to do certain things for the other. If I make a promise and then fail to follow-through, people can likely say that I revealed I was a phony, or not a person of my word. If I follow-through on it, then I show people I am someone who can be trusted. Or to borrow biblical language, I show that I am "true, "righteous," or "just."

Covenants were often entered into with a ceremony of sorts and the documents reflect that ceremony. It is typically in six parts: the preamble, prologue, stipulations, witnesses, sanctions, and document clause. The preamble identified the parties who were entering into the covenant or contract: "I am the Lord your God ..."The prologue gave a brief history of how the parties were connected to one another: "... who brought you out of the land of Egypt." The stipulations are the individual laws or terms of the agreement. They were what you needed to do within the contract. The witnesses are those who are watching you enter into the agreement and who will later be called on to account if you later say you didn't ever make an agreement, or you want them to account that the person you made an agreement with agreed to certain obligations. Within the Bible this is God himself or "heaven and earth," which just means all of creation. The sanctions are those blessings and curses that are meant to incentivize your behavior. In other words, they're the carrot or stick to make you keep your obligations (see, Deuteronomy 28-33). The document clause is the provision, which allows the covenant to periodically reviewed to ensure both parties are keeping their end of the deal.

All of this is extremely important in terms of giving us a context of how to understand Israel's (and our!) relationship to God. When we are reading the Law we are really reading a covenant, or an ancient contract. Again, you enter into contracts everyday without realizing it. When you rent an apartment you sign a lease agreement that lays out the terms: the landlord who owns the property is allowing you to live in their property, but under certain terms. They expect you to pay them a monthly amount of money (called "rent") and to keep the property in certain conditions. Likewise, the landlord enters into certain obligations with you as a tenant: they make themselves available to repair and fix things when needed, they ensure that the property is a livable place, and they give you something called "quiet enjoyment," which means they won't hover and coming walking in any time they want. All of these specifics are the terms of your lease. If you break that agreement, the landlord has grounds to have you evicted from their property. Likewise if the landlord breaks the agreement by not repairing things so that it is unlivable, you may have grounds to move out or not have to pay rent.

But we enter into many more contracts. Read the receipt on your dry cleaning or when you park in a public parking garage and you will notice that they're also contracts. Again, we do this on a daily basis or several times a day.

The biblical law is a contract. The specific legal codes are the terms of the agreement. After God brought the people out of Egypt he covenanted to be their unique suzerain, if they would be his loyal vassals. This covenant can be summarized in very brief language, which we often call the "Ten Commandments (see, Exodus 20:1-17)," but these Ten Commandments were fleshed out legally in the body of material we see in Exodus 20-Deuteronomy. This is how law works. As people live their lives, the details get fleshed out. Courts do this all on a daily basis and it was no different in ancient times.

Similarly, when Israel kept its terms of the contract it could be considered "loyal," "true," or "righteous." When God was faithful to his contract he was also "righteous," "loyal," "faithful," or "true." This language is found throughout the entire Old Testament and informs what people are saying and doing on almost every page. For example, the Psalmist can pray for God to show his righteousness after he recounts how he has kept his end of the deal. See the following:

Good and upright is the Lord;
therefore he instructs sinners in his ways.
9
He guides the humble in what is right
and teaches them his way.
10
All the ways of the Lord are loving and faithful
toward those who keep the demands of his
covenant.

11

For the sake of your name, Lord,
forgive my iniquity, though it is great.

12

Who, then, are those who fear the Lord?
He will instruct them in the ways they should
choose.

13

They will spend their days in prosperity,
and their descendants will inherit the land.

14

The Lord confides in those who fear him;
he makes his covenant known to them.

Turn to me and be gracious to me,
for I am lonely and afflicted.

17

Relieve the troubles of my heart
and free me from my anguish.

18

Look on my affliction and my distress
and take away all my sins.

19

See how numerous are my enemies
and how fiercely they hate me!

20

Guard my life and rescue me;
do not let me be put to shame,
for I take refuge in you.

21

May integrity and uprightness protect me,
because my hope, Lord, is in you.

22
Deliver Israel, O God,
*   from all their troubles!*

Here, David is appealing to his suzerain. Notice the language: "upright," "true," etc. David equates these qualities of God with his covenant (Ps 25:10, 14). This covenant is God's ways or paths – i.e., the path he instructed Israel to walk down through his servant Moses. David is surrounding by enemies, but he knows that some of God's contracted obligations are to deliver Israel from their enemies. Since David is part of Israel, he's therefore entitled to lay claim to these promises. While he admits his weakness, he also has sought to be loyal to his covenant obligations. As he says it "may integrity and uprightness protect me…" In other words, "God I am weak, but I have sought to be faithful, please do your part and show me you are faithful or true by destroying my enemies like you promised us long ago."

Israel's Contract, Not Ours
A few very important things follow from this. First, you and I as Christians, are not under this contract, but a different one. Towards the end of Israel's history, God promised through the prophets Jeremiah and Ezekiel that he would make a "new covenant" (See, Jeremiah 31:31-34 and Ezekiel 36:26-27).

Paul in his letters elaborates on this quite a bit. We will deal more with this when we discuss how to read Paul's letters, but suffice it to say Paul has quite a bit to say in Romans and Galatians about faith v. "the works of the Law." Since the Protestant reformation, many have read this phrase to be about earning our salvation, but if we read Paul carefully, we will see that he has something much more specific in mind. Again, remember Paul had a unique commission, which was to bring the gospel to non-Jews (Gal 1:15). In this role, he told his Gentile converts that they didn't need to keep these covenant stipulations (what he means by "the works of the Law"). Instead, he said that Gentiles and Jews alike become God's people by their faith (Gal 3:1-6). This means a Gentile doesn't need to live a Jewish, Law observant lifestyle. They can instead live a Gentile lifestyle. For Paul, this was exactly why Jesus died (Gal 2:14-21). Remember, God had promised in Genesis 12:1-3 that he wanted to bless the Gentiles. Paul's argument is that blessing the Gentiles meant they needed to remain Gentiles, not become Jews through observing the Law. Furthermore, Jesus' death and resurrection marked the beginning of a new era since it ushered in this new covenant. For his opponents to say Gentiles needed to obey the Law was tantamount to saying Jesus died for nothing (Gal 2:21). In addition, Paul explains that the Law was like a babysitter that God put in charge of his child Israel until he came of age (Gal 3:1-29). This coming of age happened with Jesus, which means:

There is neither Jew nor Gentile, neither slave nor free, nor is there male and female, for you are all one in Christ Jesus. 29 If you belong to Christ, then you are Abraham's seed, and heirs according to the promise.

In other words, God is not just a God of Jews only, but of Gentiles also (Romans 3:29-31). In Jesus, the period of the Law has come to an end and all are welcome to be who they are, whether Jew or Gentile, slave or free, male or female, and all of these people are the true sons and daughters of Abraham – i.e., true covenant partners.

This is also where Paul gets into his discussion about flesh v. spirit. Flesh refers to circumcision and physical descent from Abraham, while Spirit refers to the promise to Abraham. His Jewish-Christian opponents insisted that his converts were not true sons and daughters of Abraham unless they took on this mark in their flesh through circumcision. Paul argues vehemently that's simply not the case because the true son of Abraham wasn't born through the flesh, but God's promise, just like his converts who were made heirs by the Spirit (Gal 3:1-6). We could go on and on.

For our purposes here, just know you are not under this covenant, but a new one. This leads to our next point: some of the old law gets carried over into the new one, but not all of it. Learning to distinguish what is carried over and what isn't is learning to become a perceptive reader of the New Testament.

Lastly, while God's Law to Israel is not his Law to us, it is still his word and still teaches us important things about our God. It teaches us his holiness, his righteousness, and the types of things that matter to him. This is where the Prophets become so valuable as we will explain in later chapters.

Tips on How to Read the Law

There are a handful of common ways in which Old Testament writers, write out their legal material. Let's talk about the most important ones, before we conclude this chapter.

Casuistic Law

Also known as "Case Law," this is by far the most common. It is typically written in an "If .... Then ..." pattern. Consider Exodus 21:18-19:

If men quarrel and one hits the other with a stone or with his fist and he does not die, but is confined to bed

Then the one who struck the blow will not be held responsible if the other gets up and walks around outside with his staff; however, he must pay the injured man for the loss of his time and see that he is completely healed.

Apodictic Law

Also known as "Absolute law," apodictic law expresses commands and prohibitions in absolute terms. Within this category, the most common is the *prohibition*, which expresses a negative command: "You shall not ..." (See, Exod 20:13). A less common form of this type of law is known as the *admonition*, which expresses a positive command: "Honor your father and mother!" (See, Exod 20:12). Both of these give commands without any implication of an exception.

Conclusion

Remember, that the Law is essentially a contract between God and his people, Israel. You are currently under a new contract, but becoming familiar and learning the old contract is essential to gaining a complete picture of God. As New Covenant (Contract) Christians, we are very acquainted with God's mercy and love, but learning his Old Contractual terms will help us see what he values, and what values he is trying to grow within us through His Spirit. Understanding this contractual context will also help us get a clearer picture of what He has been trying to accomplish in history.

CHAPTER 4

The Prophets: Contract Policemen

The Old Testament Prophets are the following: Isaiah, Jeremiah, Ezekiel, Daniel, Hosea, Amos, Micah, Joel, Obadiah, Jonah, Nahum, and Habakkuk. When we come to these books, we arrive at one of the most familiar portions of the Old Testament. Just ask any beginning student of the New Testament and they will tell you that the prophets are those who foretold the coming of Jesus. In fact, that is primarily their job! To foretell the future: the coming of Jesus, the end of the world, and much, much more. It is for this reason that we can study them to learn about the end of the world or even current events.

But is this so? While the statement about the coming of Jesus is certainly true, are their jobs *primarily to predict the future?* Fee and Stuart in their marvelous little book, <u>How To Read The Bible For All Its Worth</u> point out the following:

- Less than 2% of the Prophets predicts the coming of Jesus
- Less than 5% of the Prophets describes the New Covenant age

But if their job is to predict the future, why do they do so little of it? Well, while prediction is an important part of their role, most of the future that they predict *was their future, but is now our past.* In other words, they aren't as concerned with the distant future, but their recent future. This is because *their primary job is not to predict the future, but to enforce the covenant or contract God made with Israel.* Their ability to predict the future serves this larger end. Let me explain.

The Prophets as Spokespersons

Remember what we just learned about God's Law: that at its heart is his unique covenant, or contract, that he entered into with Israel. Please also remember that this is part of that great story that God first announced in Genesis 12:1-3:

The Lord had said to Abram, "Go from your country, your people and your father's household to the land I will show you.

"I will make you into a great nation,
    and I will bless you;
I will make your name great,
    and you will be a blessing.

I will bless those who bless you,
    and whoever curses you I will curse;
and all peoples on earth
    will be blessed through you."

What's important here is that little line that says he will make them into a great nation (12:2). This is part of the great story: he begins with one man, then from him creates a family, then builds that family into a great multitude. But that isn't a nation, just yet.

Instead, he commissions Moses to deliver them from Egyptian slavery (Exodus 3) and leads them to Mt. Sinai where he agrees to enter into a unique contractual relationship with them (i.e., a covenant). It is once they enter into this contractual relationship that he makes them into a nation that is his own. God himself says it this way in Exodus 19:3-6:

"This is what you are to say to the descendants of Jacob and what you are to tell the people of Israel: 4 'You yourselves have seen what I did to Egypt, and how I carried you on eagles' wings and brought you to myself. 5 Now if you obey me fully and keep my covenant, then out of all nations you will be my treasured possession. Although the whole earth is mine, 6 you [a] will be for me a kingdom of priests and a holy nation.' These are the words you are to speak to the Israelites."

While Israel would be his treasured possession, they will also be a "kingdom of priests and a holy nation." Two things are important here: first, as a "kingdom of priests" they will be holy, set apart, and mediators of God to the rest of the world. Again, remember, the ultimate goal of all this is always to bring "blessing to the nations" (Genesis 12:3). Second, once they enter into the covenant they will be a "holy nation." That is, this is when God's promise to Abraham in Genesis 12:2 will be realized. They will be a nation that is "holy" or set apart from all the other nations in the world.

Entering into covenant with all of its immense privileges also entails immense responsibility, however. Again, they will be a "holy" nation. Connected to the covenant are promised "blessings and curses", as we discussed earlier. All of these covenant blessings and curses are laid out primarily in Deuteronomy 28 and will immediately become recognizable as the substance of what the prophets are all about. Here, God reminds the people that:

If you fully obey the Lord your God and carefully follow all his commands I give you today, the Lord your God will set you high above all the nations on earth. 2 All these blessings will come on you and accompany you if you obey the Lord your God …

He then goes on to itemize the following promised blessings: life, health, prosperity, agricultural abundance, respect, and safety (Deuteronomy 28:3-12).

Similarly, He warns the people of the following:

15 However, if you do not obey the Lord your God and do not carefully follow all his commands and decrees I am giving you today, all these curses will come on you and overtake you …

And then list some of the following promised curses: death, disease, drought, dearth, danger, destruction, defeat, deportation, destitution, and disgrace (Deuteronomy 28:15-68). Again, God wants to bless his people for their loyalty or faithfulness to covenant, but these blessings are announced with a warning. If Israel does *not* obey God's Law, the blessings will stop and curses will commence.

This is where the prophets come in: they are covenant policemen. Policemen are those whom we charge with the responsibility to enforce the law. They make sure we are keeping the law whether a traffic light, or something else. The big difference though with this analogy is that the Old Testament prophets go further: they do not have the power to enforce obedience or disobedience, but the One who commissions them, can. In this sense, the prophets are *forth-tellers* or *spokes-persons* for God: they speak on His behalf, calling the erring nation back to covenant loyalty to ensure that the blessings continue, or threaten one of the promised curses if they continue to shirk the Law.

Their message often follows a common pattern: (1) the prophet identifies a specific sin of Israel (or God's love for her), and (2) a prediction of a covenant curse or blessing. This is why they don't usually predict the distant future: if their message is that *God* is the one speaking through them, the proof of that is a promise that something that will happen in the *near* future to confirm it. Giving a prediction that is in the far off future, serves no purpose for their audience because they are unable to confirm or deny that the promised event happens.

Two very important things follow from this: first, *the content* of the prophets' message is not original. In fact, the urgency of the moment demands that the message not be original! Instead, God is summoning his people back to an ancient covenant and reminding them of what he told their forefathers generations ago: obedience means promised blessing, disobedience means promised curses. This means there are no excuses, you have heard this before and are being reminded of something I have told every generation since I brought you from Egypt to be my special people.

But this doesn't mean that the prophets aren't original *in how* they deliver their message. In fact, the prophets are often incredibly creative in how they deliver the message God has gave them. Sometimes, the prophets deliver their message by acting something out for the people to see. Ezekiel, for example, is commanded to sit destitute in the dirt and re-enact the coming besieging of Israel for all the people to see (Ezekiel 4-5). Isaiah is similarly commanded to have a child with his wife, who is also a prophetess, so that the child can be a symbol of the coming destruction of Assyria (7:10-15; 8:1-4). God tells him that before his son is old enough to know right from wrong, the Assyrians will come in to destroy the land of Israel (Isaiah 7:15; 8:3-4). He is commanded to name this child "Maher-shalal-hash-baz," which means "with the stylus of a man" because before he is old enough to hold a stylus, Assyria will be here to destroy. The child is also named "Immanuel," or "God is with us" (Isaiah 7:14) because God will be with his people to judge them, but also to preserve a remnant of them for the future (Isaiah 8:8, 10). Isaiah concludes by commanding his disciples (more on who these people are later) to write down what he is saying, and that his children are "signs" for Israel (Isaiah 8:16-17). In other words, as his children grow up they will be constant reminders that the clock on Assyria's arrival is counting down. All of this parabolic prediction is in contrast to the mediums and spiritists who are unable to predict such things (Isaiah 8:19-22).

The prophets are also creative in how they tell their message. They often use colorful and evocative language: Assyria is a mighty flood about to swirl in and drown the people (Isaiah 8:5-8), the promised blessing God will bring on Israel will be so exuberant that even the trees and mountains will sing and clap (Isaiah 55:12). In fact, it is this strongly poetic language that often lends them to be so easily misunderstood. Remember: poetry isn't literal, but symbolic. It is trying to evoke an emotion. Assyria is not *actually* a river of water, but how it *feels* when you are being forcibly drowned by a sudden, rushing river is similar to the surprise and shock that will occur when the armies of Assyria arrive to murder and kill your family. Similarly, the trees aren't *actually* going to shout and sing, but *the joy you feel* when God brings you back will be so immense it will *feel* as though the trees themselves are sharing in your joy.

Second, since the prophets are primarily *spoke-persons for God* (Exod 3:1; Isa 6; Jer 1; Ezek 1-3; Hos 1:2; Amos 7:14-15; Jonah 1:1), they are also uniquely commissioned to speak *on His behalf*. When we read the words of Isaiah, Jeremiah, Ezekiel, or the rest, we are truly hearing God himself pleading with his people to listen to him. I personally think this is what makes the prophets so exciting. Do you want to know what God really cares about? Then read the prophets! As you peel away the layers of misunderstanding and misinformation, you may be stunned at who is there beneath it all: a God who cares desperately about the poor, orphans, and widows (and surprisingly very little about sacrifices and the rest; Hosea 6:6). Civil rights leaders have nothing on the Old Testament prophets and the God who speaks through them. Also, don't expect the God you may have expected from reading theological tomes, or treatises. This God is emotionally volatile! He gets so angry he threatens to pull up his enemies skirts to expose their nakedness and wants to throw filth at them (Nahum 3:1-5), he makes one decision then quickly changes his mind because to do what he wants is too difficult and painful for him (Hosea 11:1-12, see especially verses 8-12). This is God at His most raw. He's angry, sad, tormented and underscores that this "Grand story" we are talking about is no small thing to him. He's absolutely set on his promise to Abraham and when Israel mucks it up He's furious and heartbroken. So buckle-up and get ready for a wild ride. I promise you if you begin to read the prophets, you'll begin to care less and less about whether or not this or that prophetic word is found in CNN, and much more about public policy, healthcare, and immigration.

How The Prophetic Books Are Organized And Tips On How To Read Them

Everything we discussed above gives us a context in which to read and understand the prophets, but what about how to understand their specific books? Let me say a few final things in this regard.

First, remember that the prophets are commissioned by God to speak on His behalf. So they always open with some sort of a statement that God has commissioned them (Isaiah 1:1; Jeremiah 1:1-3; Hosea 1:1; Joel 1:1; Amos 1:1; Jonah 1:1; Micah 1:1; Nahum 1:1; Habakkuk 1:1; Zephaniah 1:1; Haggai 1:1). In fact, the larger prophets go further and actually recount how God first commissioned them (Isaiah 6; Jeremiah 1:1-10; Ezekiel 1-3).

Second, the prophets delivered their message to the generation they were living in, which means that their messages were often originally delivered *orally rather than written.* We call these oral messages, oracles. Imagine then, that the various poetic oracles you are reading were probably first given orally as the prophet stood up in a crowd and shouted it to those who were listening (think of Moses in Deuteronomy for example, or Jonah's proclamation to Nineveh, Jonah 3:4).

Third, these prophets often had followers who were writing things down (Isaiah 8:16; Jeremiah 32:12, 13, 16; 36; 45:1). For example, we know from some of the narrative portions of the Old Testament that prophets often had communities that learned from them and were tasked with preserving their message (1 Samuel 10:5, 10, 19:20). It is likely these disciples who are at least partially responsible for the prophetic books that we now have. Likely, the prophet began compiling their books with the help of these disciples, or after the death of the prophet the disciple began to compile their various oracles and group them into thematic order (See, Jeremiah 36:4-8; 45). This is why their books can often be very difficult to read. Reading from one chapter to another can literally be jumping back and forth from various oracles that are now put into a single place because they deal with similar topics.

Finally, because the prophets are speaking to their immediate generation it is important that you learn some history to understand them. Don't worry, this isn't too difficult and there are often great resources for you to do so. Just know that some of the specific things they are referring to will make better sense once you learn a little bit about what is going on in their own time.

Conclusion

The prophets were contract policemen. They were God's spokespersons who were speaking on His behalf to summon the people back to covenant loyalty by reminding them of promised blessings and warning them of promised curses. This was an emotional message, and not for the faint of heart. Jeremiah is one of my personal favorites because he tells us about the emotional toll this took on his life. He was a priest who had been summoned to be a prophet (Jeremiah 1:1). This means he had spent most of his life learning to feel sympathy for people's weaknesses and frailties so he can represent men to God. Yet, God called him to be a prophet who had to represent God to men. This means he often had to deliver stern warnings to people he deeply loved. The result was a very conflicted man, who lived his life in emotional turmoil (see, his "confessions" in 11:18-12.6; 15:10-21; 17:14-18; 18:23; 20:7-18). In one of these he analogizes his divine commission as being like that of a young woman who had been seduced and subsequently "overpowered" (i.e., raped. See, Jeremiah 20:7). In other words, his initial prophetic summons felt like a young suitor wooing him with grand overtures, but he felt it was all with the aim of "overpowering" him against his will. He goes on to explain that he often promises himself he will no longer speak God's messages, and then the prophetic "word" comes to him and feels compelled to speak (20:8-9). It was utter turmoil.

But why would God do this? Again, the prophet represented God. *God* was in emotional turmoil. He had already destroyed the Northern Kingdom through the Assyrians (as Isaiah had prophesied) and now the Southern Kingdom was on the verge of going to Babylon. Exile was eminent, which was the ultimate covenant curse. God was devastated and pleading with his erring nation to listen and change course. Thus, the emotional turmoil of a kind-hearted priest forced to convey a message of judgment, mirrored a kind-hearted God forced to tell his people judgment was coming. His entire plan and promise to Abraham were on the line and He was crushed and conflicted.

Again, you've been warned. Don't read the prophets if you don't want your life changed! It may be tough at first, but you will see your God in a whole new light: He is fiery, passionate, and even emotional. As you see this you will begin to appreciate what He cares so much about and why those things are so important to Him. You will also begin to be more appreciative of your own emotional life. Remember, you're made in His image and when you become enraged or despondent, you're just like Him. Draw close, but prepare to be changed.

CHAPTER 5

The Wisdom Books: Listening to Lady Wisdom

The Wisdom books are all of the following: Proverbs, Job, and Ecclesiastes. These books are unique in that they do not mention any of what seems to be foundational to the rest of the Bible: there is no mention of Abraham, the promises to the ancestors, the Exodus, the covenant with Moses, the importance of Jerusalem, the Davidic dynasty, and more. Why is this? Well, to answer this question we will need to briefly step back and explain a little about how these books view the world, and then we'll provide some helpful tips on how to interpret them.

First, we must mention that there is a pronounced difference between Proverbs and the other two books. The book of Proverbs is what may be called "basic wisdom," while Job and Ecclesiastes presuppose you already know how the wisdom in Proverbs works and then builds on it. Because of this, Job and Ecclesiastes are sometimes referred to as "complex wisdom." We will begin then first with Proverbs and basic wisdom, and then move on to how Job and Ecclesiastes take these ideas and elaborate on them to deal with more challenging questions.

Basic Wisdom

First and foremost, the wisdom tradition starts with creation. Rather than situating things in covenant, the wisdom literature and the sages who wrote them, instead situated questions in the context of God's work in the created order. This does not mean covenant isn't important to them – we will see numerous places where it is very clear that it is still in the background – but it means that they took seriously the fact that the God who covenanted with them, was first and foremost the Creator of the whole world. This truth, they felt, had very important implications, and is largely why they don't expressly mention Abraham, Moses or the others foundational biblical ideas.

The first important implication of this creation based worldview is that someone can learn lessons from how the world "works." In other words, we can all observe that there are definite consequences to living life a certain way, and these consequences are there by the Creator's design. As one writer aptly put it: "the hard facts of life are God's facts, and they are there to knock the nonsense out of us." There are dozens of examples: laziness ends in poverty, but hard work brings wealth (Proverbs 6:6-11; 10:4; 12:27; 26:15), smart people choose their friends carefully (Proverbs 12:26) and look for people who keep their secrets (Proverbs 16:28; 17:9) are reliable in hard times (Proverbs 17:17; 18:24) and can forgive their slights (Proverbs 17:9), while foolish people mistakenly trust people who talk to much (Proverbs 20:19) and come to ruin (18:24).

These things are there for all of us to see. In fact, Wisdom is personified as a woman who shouts to us everyday as we go about our business. Note the following in Proverbs 1:20-33:

Out in the open wisdom calls aloud,
    she raises her voice in the public square;
21
on top of the wall[d] she cries out,
    at the city gate she makes her speech:
22
"How long will you who are simple love your simple ways?
    How long will mockers delight in mockery

and fools hate knowledge?
23
Repent at my rebuke!
    Then I will pour out my thoughts to you,
    I will make known to you my teachings.
24
But since you refuse to listen when I call
    and no one pays attention when I stretch out my
hand,
25
since you disregard all my advice
    and do not accept my rebuke,
26
I in turn will laugh when disaster strikes you;
    I will mock when calamity overtakes you—
27
when calamity overtakes you like a storm,
    when disaster sweeps over you like a whirlwind,
    when distress and trouble overwhelm you.
28
"Then they will call to me but I will not answer;
    they will look for me but will not find me,
29
since they hated knowledge
    and did not choose to fear the Lord.
30
Since they would not accept my advice
    and spurned my rebuke,
31
they will eat the fruit of their ways
    and be filled with the fruit of their schemes.
32

For the waywardness of the simple will kill them,
   and the complacency of fools will destroy them;
33
but whoever listens to me will live in safety
   and be at ease, without fear of harm."

Notice that Wisdom here isn't shouting to us at church, but "out in the open," "in the public square," "on the city wall," and "at the city gate" (Proverbs 1:22). In other words, when you drive to work, when you're shopping at the grocery store, when you overhear that conversation of a person who feels betrayed by their friend – in all of these little moments you see things daily that counsel you: "be wise! Don't act like this person or make the same mistake!" This is Lady Wisdom pleading with you to be smart (See also, Proverbs 8:1-22; 9:4-6).

For this reason, the sages in the wisdom literature will draw our attention to obvious things we see every day and ask us to consider their lesson: ants for the lazy person (Proverbs 6:6-11), the promiscuous young man who falls for a woman who ruins his reputation (Proverbs 7:6-27), and many more.

Second, and an even more profound lesson follows from this, when we hear Lady Wisdom, *we are really hearing God Himself*, since he is the One who Created the world with His Wisdom and Understanding (Proverbs 8:22-31). This is also why choosing to be wise, means choosing to fear the God who made the world this way (Proverbs 1:7). This is very important and absolutely essential to understanding how the wisdom books work: when you see how life has consequences and choose to make smart choices in light of that, you are really making the choice to respect and fear the God who put those consequences in place (Proverbs 1:7; 9:10; 10:27). This is why being wise, also means being righteous (Proverbs 9:9; 11:30; 23:24), upright (15:7), or fearing God (1:7; 9:10; 10:27) and is why the fool is considered immoral (Proverbs 10:21, 23). He sees these God-created consequences, and mocks them by insisting on still doing what he wants (Proverbs 1:22; 14:9; 19:29). Not only is that showing disrespect to the God who made the world this way, it is also immensely foolish since he or she will only end up ruining their own lives in the process (1:22-33; 9:13-18; 10:8, 10; 13:3; 18:24). The wisdom literature doesn't want this to happen to you! It wants you to be smart so you can have a wonderful life with good friends (Proverbs 12:26; 28; 17:9, 17; 18:24; 20:19), a happy marriage (Proverbs 5; 7), financial security (Proverbs 3:16; 8:18, 21; 12:27; 13:8; 14:20; 21:17; 22:4) and more.

But it also goes even further than this: choosing to fear God and make smart choices, also means you will come to know God better (Proverb 2:5). You will attain "the knowledge of God," because you will begin to see the world from his perspective, and come to appreciate that a wise life is also the best way to live. You will also be learning to "Trust the Lord with all your heart" (Proverbs 22:17-19) and applying wisdom to every area of your life rather than relying on your own understanding – with the result that your life will be much easier, it'll feel like you're walking down a straight, smooth road rather than a crooked one that is always changing, and filled with rocks that make you trip and fall (Proverbs 3:5-6). In other words, learning to fear God (Proverbs 1:7), knowing God (Proverbs 2:5), and trusting God (Proverbs 3:5; 22-17-19) are connected to living a wise life. Furthermore, living a wise, smart life is an act of devotion to your God and a tool to draw closer to Him. God, through Lady Wisdom, is pleading with you to make smart choices with your money, choice of friends, marital faithfulness and a lot more!

Finally, since Wisdom is part of the created order, it is there for all to see, even non-covenant members. Notice for example, that Job is described as "living among the people of the East" and "in the land of Uz (Job 1:1-3). That is, he is not a part of Israel, but probably an Edomite on the East side of the Jordan River (See, Lamentation 4:21). Note also that Proverbs 30:1-4 and 31:1-9 are collections by non-Israelites. In fact, many scholars have long recognized that Proverbs 22:17-24:22 is remarkably similar to the Egyptian Instruction of Amenemopet. This may surprise you, but it is nothing to be afraid of, and directly follows from what we as God's people believe. Again, since the God who has entered into a unique covenant with us is also the Creator of the world, his wisdom is there for everyone to see. This also provides some common ground with our non-Christian friends: they can still make smart financial choices, and give us wise advice about choosing friends. It doesn't mean we agree on everything, but wisdom is wisdom – wherever we find it.

Lastly, this also means that how we live has real consequences. See, you cannot separate your daily living from your faith in God, and how wisely we live our lives has implications for how well we know God. "Godly" people who constantly make bad choices, aren't really all that godly. In fact, it shows that they do not yet "Trust" or "Fear" God in that area of their lives, which is why they are constantly plagued with frustrations. Wisdom is a life-long pursuit, but God wants us to know Him there too.

Proverbs

So, real quick, how does Proverbs flesh this out for us?

First, we have an initial prologue that tells us what the book is all about (Proverbs 1:1-7):

for gaining wisdom and instruction;
  for understanding words of insight;
3
for receiving instruction in prudent behavior,
  doing what is right and just and fair;
4
for giving prudence to those who are simple,
  knowledge and discretion to the young—
5
let the wise listen and add to their learning,
  and let the discerning get guidance—
6
for understanding proverbs and parables,
  the sayings and riddles of the wise.

What follows is an introduction that basically lays out what we just discussed, namely that Wisdom is calling to us and was with God when he created the world (Proverbs 8:1-36). This is from Proverbs 1:8-9:18. Again, this is meant to orient us to the collection of proverbs that follow.

We then have several "collections" of proverbs, or wise sayings. The first is from 10:1-22:16, then 22:17-24:34, and a collection of Hezekiah in 25:1-29:27, the words of Agur in 30:1-33; the words of Lemuel in 31:1-9; and a final conclusion of Lady Wisdom as a godly wife in 31:10-31.

Tips On How To Read Proverbs

A proverbs is "a concise, memorable statement of truth" learned over extended human experience. In other words, they are observations about life, put in a short and memorable way. This means that they are *not* promises. For example, when someone says, "the early bird catches the worm" it simply means that *typically* a person who wakes up early to work hard will often be successful, but not that they will be in every single instance. We can all think of the times in our life when we have worked very hard for something and it didn't work out, but that doesn't mean we stop working hard. Nine times out of ten, working hard does pay off so it is the *wise* way to live life. It just isn't a promise. In that same way, we cannot quote the biblical proverbs and expect them to be promises. Again, they are *wise sayings* and *observations about life.*

Complex Wisdom

Complex wisdom assumes the conversation and ideas found in basic wisdom: God as the Creator, wise observations, and the rest. The difference is that Job and Ecclesiastes deal with the problem of what happens when someone seeks to live a wise life and it doesn't turn out well. In other words, if the Proverbs say: "Do this and you'll be blessed" Job and Ecclesiastes come along and say: "I tried, and I wasn't."

Here is the hard truth: bad things sometimes do happen to good people. Sometimes we make wise choices and it just doesn't turn out well for us. We invest our money in something that looks prudent, but we end up losing it all or we develop a friendship with someone who seems trustworthy, but we get burned in the end. Life is hard and it doesn't always turn out well. So how do we square this with living a wise life? Let's look first at Ecclesiastes and then finish with Job.

Ecclesiastes

The writer of Ecclesiastes stands within the Wisdom tradition and its approach to God, but questions many of its assumptions. He sees life as incredibly complex and full of contradictions and uses the word absurd or meaningless to capture this (1:2; 12:8). This means that the wise sayings in Proverbs are too simplistic for him. As we mentioned, he reasons that sometimes things don't work out for us. For example, sometimes we work hard, but it doesn't always pay off so there must be more to the story.

He goes further and observes something he likes to call "The work of God," and the "burden," or "evil" God has laid on men (See, 1:12-14; 3:10, 11; 7:23-25, 27-28; 8:9, 16-17; 11:5. This "work of God" and "burden" is a two-sided coin: on the one hand, it refers to this overwhelming element to life; it is often too big and too tough to understand (8:16-17). This is because God, the Creator, has prescribed certain boundaries for us. For example, He has determined our "times and seasons" (3:1-8) and, though everything is "beautiful" in its time (3:11), we are often unable to understand when it happens. In its place human experience is one of endless repetition (1:3-11; 3:1-8, 15). How many of us can dispute that? Think about the majority of how your time is spent: you wake up, get the kids ready for school, go to work, and repeat. Even your weekends are spent doing chores, cleaning your room, running errands, and so on. Yes, we have wonderful moments and memories, but the vast majority of our time is spent doing monotonous things. Our experience is also full of "absurdities:" those things that just don't make any sense. Times in our life when it seems things just don't work out or bad things happen to good people (See, 1:2; 12:8; 1:14; 2:11, 15, 17, 23, 26; 4:4, 7, 8, 16; 5:7). Again, we all have had that. Those moments a dear friend of yours is diagnosed with cancer and you wonder, "Why would God take that beautiful mother from her kids?" Secretly, if we're honest, we've all wished He would choose that jerk we work with instead. It's disheartening and confusion.

The other side of this "burden" God has placed on men is that it makes the writer of Ecclesiastes feel like all of our hard work and careful choices don't really amount to much. Over and over again he asks the question: "what does the worker gain from his toil?" (1:3; 3:9) and "who knows what will happen after him?" (See, 3:22; 6:12; 7:14; 8:7; 10:14). His point is that if we're honest none of us really knows. As he himself says in 8:16-17:

16 When I applied my mind to know wisdom and to observe the labor that is done on earth—people getting no sleep day or night— 17 then I saw all that God has done. No one can comprehend what goes on under the sun. Despite all their efforts to search it out, no one can discover its meaning. Even if the wise claim they know, they cannot really comprehend it.

And isn't that true? Yes, we have faith there is more, but the hard truth is none of us have been to heaven and come back to talk about it. We are living by faith.

So what does he tell us to do in light of this? This is where his wise teaching comes in: first, he thinks human beings needs to let go of trying to figure it all out! God's ways are inscrutable and no one knows the answer to things (8:1, 16-17). As hard as it is, he counsels us to accept this part of life (11:3-5).

Second, he sees the "fear of God" differently than the sages of basic wisdom. Remember that for them it means respect for the inherent cause and effect reality of the created order. The sages of basic wisdom argued that If God made things this way, than by choosing to make smart choices in light of that, was to "Fear God." Not so for Ecclesiastes! Instead, for him he looks out at the incomprehensibility of life and is *afraid*. He realizes that life doesn't have any guarantees: the devoted house wife may be hit by a drunk driver and end up paralyzed, the godly parents may have a child with a debilitating illness, the diligent business man may end up losing everything in a financial crash. This is scary! He sees God involved in this. We often don't want to talk about this, but the truth is these things do happen, and if we believe God is sovereign, *he is allowing it to happen. This* then is what he means by fear God. He wants you to look at the hard truth that you are not in control of your own life: you didn't choose when and how you would be born, you also don't get to choose when and how you'll die, or what will happen to you on any given day (Ecclesiastes 3:1-11). God does. This means we need to have a healthy fear of Him because He can give and He can take away from us whatever He wants, and whenever He wants. Fear God means simply: be afraid of a God this powerful!

Third, since none of us can escape life's endless repetition and the futility that it implies, we need to humbly accept our lot and find enjoyment in our work (2:24-26; 3:12-13, 22; 5:18-20; 8:15; 9:7-10). It means learning to take things a day at a time and learning to live in the present, because "no man knows what is coming, and so all may be gone tomorrow" (see, 9:1-12; 11:7-12:7). It's also why he ends his book advising the young (11:7-12:7). In a beautiful poem that personifies the different part of the human body as it ages and then dies, he urges young people to go out and live their lives (11:9-10, 12:1). While reminding them that God will one day judge them as a way of tempering their choices, he urges them to "follow the ways of your heart and whatever your eyes see." In other words: be young! Again, this is just true, isn't it? We often say youth is wasted on the young and there is truth to that. Look, if one day you will age and become frail and even die, now is the time to do the things you won't be able to do later! Climb trees, go on hikes, travel the world, fall in love, and make mistakes! Living your life this way is showing God that you're afraid of him because you know it can all change in a moment. God has given you life, and He wants you to go out there and live it! Doing that means you "remember your Creator" (12:1, 6).

Job

Job is a gorgeous book. It is also a fairly complicated one. Let me first provide a brief outline of Job so we can get the big picture and then I'll explain what I think it is trying to tell us.

I. Introduction (1.1-2.13):

i. 1.1-5: Prologue

ii. 1.6-22: Job's first test: 'Does job fear God for nothing?' (1.9)

iii. 2.1-10: Job's second test: 'A man will give all he has for his own life – stretch out your hand and he will curse you to your face!' (2.4)

iv. 2.11-13: Job's three friends

II. Disputations (3.1-42.6): Job pours out his complaint and is corrected

i. First cycle:

1. 3.1-26: Job speaks: curses the day of his birth

2. 4.1-5.27: Eliphaz

3. 6.1-7.21: *Job responds*

4. 8.1-22: Bildad

5. 9.1-10.22: *Job replies*

6. 11.1-20: Zophar

7. 12.1-14.22: *Job replies*

ii. Second cycle:

1. 15.1-35: Eliphaz

2. 16.1-17.16: *Job replies*

3. 18.1-21: Bildad

4. 19.1-29: *Job replies*

5. 20.1-29: Zophar

6. 21.1-34: *Job replies*

iii. Third cycle:

1. 22.1-30: Eliphaz

2. 23.1-24.25: *Job replies*

3. 25.1-6: Bildad

4. 26.1-31.40: *Job replies*

III.   32.1-4: Apparent resolution/interlude:

i.   Fourth cycle:

1. 32.5-37.24: Elihu

2. 38.1-40.5: God's first confrontation; Job's first response

3. 40.6-42.6: God's second confrontation; Job's second response

IV.   Epilogue (42.7-16):

This outline helps us see what the book is all about. First, the prologue raises the key question: do we serve God for its own sake or because we get something for it (1:9; 2:4-5)? You see, if we say that God blesses the righteous and curses the wicked (like Proverbs implies) then it is easy to say we should fear God to get the good stuff, and not do it because it is the right thing to do. Job poses the question: what happens if God removes those good things, will we still maintain our piety (See, 2:3, 9 "maintain his integrity" 2.3)? Within the dialogues Job continues to maintain that he does indeed keep his integrity (27.5; 31.6), but he is troubled that he is suffering when he has done nothing wrong. In language reminiscent of a courtroom, he demands that God hear his complaint. His friends view his insistence that he's doing nothing wrong as "undermining" piety and hinder[ing] devotion to God" (15.4). This is because if God allows the righteous to suffer like this, people wouldn't fear him – since what's the point? God is also a little bothered by it and says that Job is "darkening my counsel" (38.2) and "discredit[ing] my justice and . . . condemn[ing] me to justify yourself" (40.8).

The ultimate answers are in the two appearances of God to Job in 38-42:6. Here, rather than answering Job's questions God instead assaults Job with even more questions. Again and again, Job has to admit that he doesn't know the answers to how God created the world or keeps it orderly. The point is that just as you do not know how the Creator keeps the physical order to things, so you don't know how he keeps the moral order. In other words, it isn't your place to ask, "Why?" It certainly isn't the answer that either Job or us want, but it is a good one.

Essentially, Job never really answers our questions. On the one hand, it tells us that we have to be committed to keep our integrity and do the right thing, because God as our Creator is worthy of it, not because we want the reward. On the other hand, He does indeed reward the righteous and curse the wicked, but when and how He does this is entirely up to Him. We may be blessed or we may not. God is free to do what He wants and when He wants.

Conclusion

Life is complex and there aren't any easy answers. Generally, we will find that approaching life with the guidance of basic wisdom, we are able to make wise choices. Through it we will grow more cautious in our relationships, more prudent with our money, and more attuned to how our decisions have real consequences in our lives. The sages remind us that growing in this awareness is really about growing in our relationship with the Creator who made life this way.

Sometimes, though, we may go through times in our lives when we re-examine our choices, and can honestly say we would have still made the decisions we did – but things didn't work out well. We feel the sting of a friend's betrayal, or suffer through financial hardship. This doesn't mean we were necessarily foolish, only that sometimes difficulties befall us all. This is when we can circle back to the sages of complex wisdom to remember the lessons they've taught us. Like Job, we can remind ourselves that we don't serve just when times are good, but because our God is worthy, regardless.

Finally, we can all appreciate the wisdom of Ecclesiastes. If we are honest, life can be fairly unpredictable. This should both caution us and inspire us to live each day as though it may be our last, or at least appreciate the good things we currently have – because tomorrow they can be taken away from us. As the poet reminds us, one day we will grow frail, afraid of noises and sudden movements in the street and then the spirit will return to God who gave it. The time to be afraid of God is now, go out therefore and live this beautiful life God has given while you're able to!

CHAPTER 6

The Psalms: Israel's Prayers

Even if we are not an ardent reader of the Bible, the Psalms are probably still familiar territory. In fact, I can still remember as a very young Christian, when my choice of worship songs still involved listening to "Stand By Me" by Ben E. King, that the Psalms electrified me. Whether it was feeling the emotional resonance of joy in Psalm 5, or feeling similarly in need of God's intervention in Psalm 25, it almost perfectly captured and gave language to what I was feeling.

Perhaps one of the most emotional, and humbling moments in my life, was when I lived in Israel and was able to hike out and spend the night in some of the caves David hid out in when he fled from Saul. I can remember reading the various Psalms he had penned during that time and wondered how alone and afraid he must have felt. Little did he know that these were the moments in his life when God was preparing him to be a compassionate King after God's own heart.

In fact, Fee and Stuart in their excellent book <u>How To Read The Bible For All Its Worth</u>, state the following:

The problem with interpreting the Psalms arises primarily from their nature – what they are. Because the Bible is God's Word, most Christians automatically assume that all it contains are words from God to people. Thus many fail to recognize that the Bible also contains words spoken to God or about God, and these words, too, are God's Word.

I think this is very true, and I certainly couldn't have said it better. One of the very unique things about the Bible is that it isn't simply God's Word *to* us, but also provides us with some guidance on *how to talk to God.* I think this is why we often identify so much with it. As I just mentioned, as a young Christian it perfectly captured my joy and anxiety and gave me language to express that to God. When I was young I didn't have the emotional maturity yet to often even know what I was feeling, much less know how to tell God about it – but the Psalms gave me guidance. How incredible is that? I can tell you that even now as an adult, I often still don't always know what I'm feeling or how to articulate my feelings, but the Psalms are here to give us guidance.

Suffice it to say then: the Psalms pack a lot of emotional weight and are a treasure trove for us in our pursuit of God. But how are we to read them and apply them to our lives?

I think the best place to start in terms of getting our bearings on the Psalms is to understand how they were written and compiled. From there we will move on to provide some specific guidance on its use of poetic language and different sub-genres of psalms.

The Psalms: A Collection Within A Collection

When I was young, I remember thinking that the Psalms were akin to a journal. I imagined King David penning these beautiful songs in the agony of those caves. This is partially true, but doesn't give us the whole picture.

The Psalms are actually a collection of books: five to be exact. Each "book" has an introductory statement and a concluding doxology. Book one comprises Psalms 1-41 (Psalms 1:1; 41:13), book two Psalms comprises Psalms 42-72 (Psalm 42:1; 71:18-19), book three comprises Psalms 73-89 (Psalms 73:1; 89:52), book four comprises Psalms 90-106 (Psalm 90:1; 106:48), and book five comprises Psalms 107-150 (Psalm 107:1; 150). Additionally, it seems that at least at some point, these five books were considered a single book or at least a single collection. We can see this by the way the first two Psalms (Psalms 1-2) seem to serve as an introduction and the final six (Psalms 146-150) serve as a conclusion.

This tells us that the Psalms are a *collection* and that someone has compiled the various songs within them.

Who would have done this? Well, remember that within ancient Israel there was a central place of worship – first at the temporary tent, or tabernacle, and then at the Temple in Jerusalem. Throughout its history there were different temples. The first was constructed by Solomon, but was destroyed by the Babylonians in 586 BC. It was then reconstructed when the exiles returned after seventy years. This reconstruction had much to be desired, however, and was expanded on by Herod the Great just before the birth of Jesus. Regretfully, this temple was destroyed in 70 AD when the Romans destroyed Jerusalem and scattered the Jewish people.

We know that at least a large portion of the Psalms were collected and compiled prior to the people leaving for Babylon. We know this because David himself wrote many of the Psalms (Psalm 3:1; 4:1; 5:1; 6:1; 7:1; 8:1; 9:1; 12:1; etc) and at least a portion of the collection was termed "the prayers of David son of Jesse" (72:20). Yet we also know that not all of the Psalms were written during his lifetime, because some of them at least reference the Babylonians coming in and destroying the city and the temple in 586. Psalm 137 is a classic example:

By the rivers of Babylon we sat and wept
*   when we remembered Zion.*
2
There on the poplars
*   we hung our harps,*
3

for there our captors asked us for songs,
   our tormentors demanded songs of joy;
   they said, "Sing us one of the songs of Zion!"
4
How can we sing the songs of the Lord
   while in a foreign land?
5
If I forget you, Jerusalem,
   may my right hand forget its skill.
6
May my tongue cling to the roof of my mouth
   if I do not remember you,
if I do not consider Jerusalem
   my highest joy.
7
Remember, Lord, what the Edomites did
   on the day Jerusalem fell.
"Tear it down," they cried,
   "tear it down to its foundations!"
8
Daughter Babylon, doomed to destruction,
   happy is the one who repays you
   according to what you have done to us.
9
Happy is the one who seizes your infants
   and dashes them against the rocks.

This tells us a couple things. First, at least a large portion of the Psalms were originally written by David, but were then compiled and collected for worship at the temple during Solomon's reign. Second, though David did write many of them, there were other contributors: there are the songs/or psalms "of the Sons of Korah" (Ps 42–49; 84–85; 87–88), (2) the psalms and/or songs "of Asaph" (Ps 50; 73–83) and (3) the songs "of ascents" (Ps 120–134).Third, at least some of the work of compiling and collecting the Psalms continued when the people returned from Babylon. This is why we have Psalms like Psalm 137 that were penned during this heartbreaking period in the nation's history.

The Psalms then are a collection. Each Psalm was likely originally penned by a person or group of people (David, the sons of Korah, sons of Asaph, etc). Some of these, as I referenced, probably were akin to a journal. So, for example, we know that David penned many Psalms when he was in hiding from Saul (Psalms 18:1; 52:1; 54:1; 57:1; 59:1). These very personal songs were then collected and included in a book (book one or two of what is now our Book of Psalms). This is when the small notes before the Psalms, often referred to as "superscriptions," were likely added. These superscriptions tend to fall into a few broad categories: (1) author, (2) name of collection, (3) type of psalm, (4) musical notations, (5) liturgical notations and (6) brief indications of occasion for writing.

These superscriptions provide information for the worshiper and the worship leaders at the temple.

Perhaps the best way to understand the book of Psalms then is something akin to a hymnal. Hymnals also typically contain songs written by individuals, but then collected and compiled in a collection. Those songs may represent decades or hundreds of years of individuals' experiences with God. The difference is that this hymnal originally was used at the Temple in Jerusalem, and therefore, reflects the life of God's people under the Old Covenant/contract. We should expect, therefore, that it gives language to the theology and worldview we have already discussed in our introduction to the Law and the Prophets. It also will give expression to how people during this time worshipped God. We will talk a little about each of this before wrapping up our conversation on the Psalms.

A few important lessons for interpreting the Psalms immediately follows, however. First, we can look at an individual Psalm in terms of its original historic context – David hiding from king Saul, for example. Second, we can look and see how the persons who have collected the Psalms have organized them to hint at how they read or heard them. Let me explain. The Psalms are often organized around specific themes or ideas: Psalm 93-100 has the recurring refrain "The Lord reigns" in 93:1; 96:10; 97:1;99:1; Ps 111–118 are a series of "Hallelujah psalms"; Ps 138–145 all include "of David" in their titles, and Ps 146–150 their frequently include the phrase "Praise the Lord." There is also a group called the "Great Hallel" from Psalms 120–136. But the organization seems to go even deeper: sometimes the Psalms appear to be organized into a logical order where an issue raised in one Psalm is addressed in another. One can see this in the progression from Psalm 2 through the next several Psalms that follow. This occurs in several other places as well. By being able to recognize this, we can see that the editors and organizers of the different Psalms are providing us insights into how they understood them.

Specific Types of Psalms

Since a different person writes each Psalm at different times, we should expect to find different types of Psalms and this is exactly what we find. While the Psalms generally are songs or prayers, there are a few sub-genres. The most common are the following: the complaint, imprecatory psalms, psalms of thanksgiving, and wisdom psalms.

Let's talk briefly about each one.

Psalms of Complaint

The complaint is the most common genre of prayer in the psalms. This shouldn't surprise us given what we already discussed about the Law and how it was a contract, which imposed certain responsibilities on each party. Since a complaint is a heartfelt petition for Yahweh to deliver from an unsolvable crisis, it is essentially an invocation by the human covenant partner to the divine one. As we discussed earlier, this is why it is often an appeal to Yahweh to reveal his "righteousness" or "faithfulness."

For an individual the crisis may be severe illness, misfortune, or false accusations; for the community, it might be drought, plagues, or invasions by enemies. Again, none of this should surprise us since these are the various blessings and curses of the covenant laid out in Deuteronomy 28.

Psalm 22 is a classic example of the Complaint. 22:1-2 opens with an invocation of God's name as a way of making contact with Yahweh. 22:3-4 is an affirmation of confidence by which the petitioner affirms trust in God. 22:6-8 describes in general terms the affliction threatening the individual or community. 22:19-21 is the actual petition where the worshipper specifically asks God for help. Finally, complaints often close with a thanksgiving element and here it is in 22:22-26.

When the king either speaks or is spoken of, we refer to the complaint as a *royal* complaint (See, Psalm 89; 144).

Our Lord used Psalm 22 while suffering on the cross (Mark 15:34; Matthew 27:46). Remember he was a covenant member of Israel. When he invoked this Psalm of Complaint, therefore, he was standing in a long line of "righteous sufferers" who cast themselves upon Yahweh's mercy and covenant righteousness for vindication. While many covenant members suffered unjustly, Jesus was distinctly innocent, calling forth God's vindication through raising him from the dead. Thus revealing that God is once and for all loyal to His covenant promises. In this sense, Jesus *fulfilled* the meaning of Psalm 22 by both offering us an example to follow and by giving us renewed hope in the God who vindicated Him.

Imprecatory Psalms

An "imprecation" is a curse. The imprecatory psalms therefore are a type of complaint where the righteous sufferer asks God to curse or destroy his enemies. Sometimes we can read these psalms and be troubled. Perhaps the most classic example is Psalm 137 and it *is* troubling one:

By the rivers of Babylon we sat and wept
*   when we remembered Zion.*

2

There on the poplars
*   we hung our harps,*

3

for there our captors asked us for songs,
*   our tormentors demanded songs of joy;*
*   they said, "Sing us one of the songs of Zion!"*

4

How can we sing the songs of the Lord
*   while in a foreign land?*

5

If I forget you, Jerusalem,
*   may my right hand forget its skill.*

6

May my tongue cling to the roof of my mouth
*   if I do not remember you,*
if I do not consider Jerusalem
*   my highest joy.*

7

Remember, Lord, what the Edomites did
*   on the day Jerusalem fell.*
"Tear it down," they cried,

"tear it down to its foundations!"
8
Daughter Babylon, doomed to destruction,
*   happy is the one who repays you*
*   according to what you have done to us.*
9
Happy is the one who seizes your infants
*   and dashes them against the rocks.*

None of us can actually condone hurting a child, much less dashing them against rocks (137:9) – so what are we to make of language like this? Well, remember that the Psalms are inspired prayers directed towards God. They help us give language to our *emotions*. Remember also what we discussed about God from the prophets. He is similarly emotional – he gets angry, is sad, and even emotionally ambivalent at times. The reason why you feel the things that you do is because you are made in His image and Likeness (Genesis 1:27).

These Psalms then aren't condoning *actually* hurting children, but condoning the messy *emotions* we can sometimes feel. Think about it: the author of Psalms 137 is remembering the tragedy of when the Babylonians came in to Israel and destroyed their city. The people of Israel had their children dashed against rocks and killed. Their women were rapped. Men taken into slavery. Israel's enemy the Edomites did nothing to help, but instead cheered the Babylonians on. This made the author angry, and he wrote this Psalms to help his people grieve and give release to these emotions. Remember: life is messy. Sometimes we fantasize about hurting those who have hurt us, or embarrassed us. Often times parents who have lost their children to sexual offenders or kidnappers feel guilty for later wishing they could find the perpetrator and kill them. While we never condone *actually* killing someone, that very real human emotion is part of who we are and in some ways justified. I can tell you if someone harmed the small children in my life whom I love deeply, part of me would certainly wish someone would do the same to them! Again, this isn't condoning violence, but it is acknowledging that we do feel these things sometimes. We don't judge ourselves for it, we simply let ourselves feel it and grieve. God is giving us these Psalms to show us precisely that. He is telling us that we can feel these things and is providing a means for us to express those feelings so we can heal.

Psalms of Thanksgiving

This psalm is closely related to the Complaint mentioned above. Through such songs, the individual or community voiced joyful gratitude to God promises of thanks. Often these promises of thanks are addressed to God, but in the presence of the believing community as a way of modeling behavior.

Psalm 30 is a great example. Psalm 30:1, 12 offers a prayer to Yahweh and verses 4-5 invites the others to join in thanksgiving and praise to God. Verses 2-3, and 6-12 explain what Yahweh has done to merit such praise.

Wisdom Psalms

As the name implies, these psalms borrow from the Wisdom literature we already discussed. Rather than focusing more on complaints or thanksgiving they tend to focus on ethical behavior such as human suffering and God's apparent injustice in tolerating it. As with the wisdom tradition, they focus more on God as Creator and ruler of the Cosmos than as Israel's redeemer.

A few examples are Psalms 1, 19, 33, 39, 49, and 127. Psalm 1 shows the common wisdom theme of the contrasting fates of the righteous and the wicked. Psalm 19 calls the worshipper to consider God's glory in the heavens, reflecting wisdom's love of creation and its empirical approach to discovering truth. Finally, Psalm 33 includes a lengthy section of instruction (33:12-19) similar to what we find from the sages in Proverbs.

A Final Word: the Psalms as Poetry

Remember what we mentioned in the Introduction about poetry. It seeks to capture emotion often in metaphorical language. Let me now elaborate a little more.

Imagery

Poets are essentially artists who paint pictures with words. This is really the key to understanding poetry. An image can be a powerful means of evoking a sensory experience in our imagination. Sometimes these images can juxtapose two ideas that at first wouldn't make sense in order to bring out a deeper meaning – Paul, for example, saying that we should be mature rather than "like children tossed about on the waves" (huh? Ephesians 4:14).

By appealing to our senses and emotions, these images compel us to see and experience their word-pictures. Think of Psalm 23:1 as one example: "the LORD is my shepherd, I shall lack nothing." Here, the Psalmist compares Yahweh's loving care to the image of a shepherd looking out for his sheep. God is not *actually* a shepherd, but we can begin to understand how He loves and cares for us by first observing and reflecting on something we can know: a shepherd with his sheep. The one concrete image helps us begin to understand something abstract like the unseen God's love for His people.

Metaphor

A metaphor compares two things by saying something *is* something else. Yahweh *is* a shepherd, His Word *is* a lamp to my feet and so on. Again, familiarity with the one helps us being to understand the other.

A metaphor works by often comparing two things that are somewhat different and showing us how they are in common. The comparison of two dissimilar things gives the metaphor its striking effect.

Simile

A simile is similar to a metaphor, but rather than saying something *is* something else the writer will use the words "like" or "as." Consider the following:

Like a lily among thorns
    is my darling among the young women.

Here, the writer compares how beautiful his lover is to a flower surrounded by thorns. Again, the writer is calling you to slow down and think about. Imagine what it feels like looking at a bush covered in thorns with one lone lily. That is how his lover stands out among all the other girls. She radiates!

Hebrew Parallelism

Remember that the Bible is an ancient book. Some forms of poetry may not be as common today. One classic example is how it uses parallelism.

Parallelism is where the second line restates what was in the first line, but in a different way. In this sense, the one line *parallels* another. Here is a simple example:

Hear the word of the Lord,
    you rulers of Sodom;
listen to the instruction of our God,
    you people of Gomorrah!

The second line simply restates what was in the first line, but in another way. Sometimes, though the parallelism can be a bit more complex. Sometimes the second line doesn't just restate what was in the first line, but contrasts it. Other times, it is a subordinate statement to the first. Other times, the first line is a general statement while the second gives a specific example.

Conclusion

The Psalms are inspired prayers and songs to help us give our emotions language before God. They often call on us to slow down and prayerfully consider the word-images that the poets create. By doing this they help us acknowledge what we're feeling whether anger, grief, joy or more. God wants us to enter into this emotional life and has provided us with a means to do it.

CHAPTER 7

The Gospels and Acts: Four Testimonies, One Truth

As Christians we are all no doubt familiar with the Gospels. Why, then, a chapter on how to read them when we've already been doing so for most of our lives? Well, because sometimes familiarity can keep us the most from hearing what something has to say. I think this is particularly true when it comes to the Gospels.

For those who aren't as familiar with the Gospels, let me make some quick general observations before jumping in. Within the New Testament we have four gospels: Matthew, Mark, Luke, and John. If we took the time to examine each of these, we would immediately see that there is an obvious disjunct between Matthew, Mark, and Luke on the one hand and John on the other. The former are almost identical in how they are organized and share lots of the same stories. For this reason, biblical scholars refer to them as the "synoptic" Gospel. "Syn" comes from the Greek work meaning "with" and "optic" is from the Greek work meaning "to see" (as in an "optical" illusion). Synoptic, therefore, means "to see with." In other words, the synoptic Gospels tend to "see" similar things.

John on the other hand is fairly unique. His Gospel is organized in a way that is very different from Matthew, Mark, and Luke and he tends to tell stories that are only in his Gospel.

You may have noticed that I also included Acts in this chapter along with the Gospels. This is because Luke and Acts are really one account in two volumes. Note that both Luke and Acts are dedicated to a man by the name of Theophilus (Luke 1:3; Acts 1:1). Writing books within the ancient was very expensive. Typically, then, a wealthy benefactor helped pay for the cost of creating the book, and writers dedicated their books to them as a way of showing their gratitude. Theophilus is likely, therefore, a wealthy Christian who is helping to fund Luke's writing. This means that when we study the Gospel of Luke, we also want to study Acts since the plot ideas Luke begins in his Gospel gets developed in Acts. We will explain more about that when we write our book on Luke and Acts in the future. Suffice it for now, we want to appreciate that Luke and Acts is really a single story in two volumes, Luke-Acts.

With that let's jump into the Gospels.

The Gospels: historical and literary accounts of Jesus

When we first look at the Gospels, we should note that they are functioning at two levels: the historical and the literary.

Historical Accounts

At the historical level is that of Jesus himself. The Gospels seek to tell us about his life, ministry, death, and resurrection. At this level we want to take into account the historical life of Jesus and will likely need to take into account the historical background of the first century. We will want to acquaint ourselves with the different sects of Judaism, the conflicts with the Roman Empire, the difference between life in the Galilee and Judea. All of this is important and can greatly help us understand the full important of what Jesus taught, and what he meant by what he said.

This is also the level where we can legitimately compare the different account to create a fuller picture. For example, when we look at the Synoptic Gospels, Jesus' ministry occurs primarily within the Galilee and appears to have a single journey to Jerusalem that results in his arrest, trial, and crucifixion. Within John's Gospel, however, Jesus has several journeys to Jerusalem. We want to be cautious, but it seems that we can confidently say that Jesus did have more than one journey to Jerusalem, which is reflected in John, and that the Synoptics have simplified their accounts. Combining these two accounts help us create an approximate time frame for Jesus' ministry as between two to three years. Without combining the accounts, it would appear his ministry last only a year or less.

We can provide other examples. The Synoptics and John all provide an immense amount of detail on the last week of Jesus' life. We know with confidence about the Triumphal Entry, the Cleansing of the Temple, and his arrest in Gethsemane, trials, and ultimate crucifixion. Comparing the different accounts helps us understand what our Lord endured and gives us intimate details about his betrayals by the disciples.

Literary Accounts: Four Testimonies, One Truth

At another level, however, is the literary element. We have to remember that Jesus himself did not write a Gospel. Instead, the Gospels are written by the Evangelists to convey his life and ministry to their different communities. When they do this they choose how to organize their accounts to bring out their interpretation of his life and ministry. This is a very important point so I want to develop it more below.

Let's begin with the obvious: we have *four* separate accounts of Jesus' life, ministry, and death. Have you ever thought about that? Why would God give us *four* accounts, rather than just a single version? Some of the early Christians thought a lot about that, and one of them in particular by the name of Tatian, decided to create a single version and called it the "Diatessaron" (meaning "through the four"). This didn't go over very well, and his work was deemed heretical. The early church reaffirmed that God did not give us one single account, but the four versions we now have.

It is this four-fold nature of the Gospels that effects how we want to approach them. Often times bible studies that focus on the Gospels will toggle back and forth between the different accounts to re-create what happened. So, for example, we may hear a sermon on the sayings of Jesus from the cross where we move back and forth from Matthew, Mark, Luke, and John. While this has merit for an inquiry into the historical life of Jesus as we just discussed, it also fundamentally *ignores* the very reality we are discussing. God did not give us a single Gospel, but four. When we go about re-creating our version or harmonizing the accounts, we are actually ignoring the Gospels *as God gave them to us.*

If you look carefully on the title page of Matthew, Mark, Luke or John, you will see that they are actually called "The Gospel *according to* …" This brings us back to what we discussed in the introduction of this book. Biblical writers have their own unique way of thinking and talking about God (biblical theology). Matthew has a unique understanding of who Jesus is, what his mission was about, why he had to die, and what the resurrection means. The same is true of Mark, Luke-Acts, and John. Combine this with the fact that they are predominantly narratives, and this means that they use their narrative accounts to express this unique understanding. When we combine their accounts, it is like taking three or four different movies and editing them together with the result that you don't actually get to enjoy any of them. Finally, remember that *God* is the one who is inspiring the human authors, this means that when we don't listen to Matthew *as Matthew*, but create our own harmonized version, we are actually not hearing what *God* is trying to tell us.

Each of these accounts is written by different Evangelists, with different reasons to write. Sometimes those purposes are clearly stated like in John (John 20:30-31), while in others we have to use what we learned about narratives to infer their purposes (we will discuss this more below). Historically, it seems clear that each account was written to different communities of Christians within the first century. Each of these communities were facing different challenges, and so, needed to hear how Jesus' ministry and teaching applied to those challenges. Again, this means that the Evangelists aren't concerned with simply relaying what Jesus taught for its own sake, but for the sake of the churches they were ministering to. We won't have time in this book to explain too much about each writer's purpose, but we will do so in future books on each of the Gospels to help you best understand their theology and the needs they were addressing.

My hope, though, is that you are curious to know things like why Luke thinks Jesus had to die. It is not the same as what Matthew thinks, or Mark, or John. In fact, did you know Luke doesn't focus much on the death of Jesus, but instead focuses on his ascension? Did you know that – according to Luke – the ascension of Jesus is partly what saves you? Luke has a lot to say about that (big hint: it is partly why he wrote Acts). Additionally, Matthew has a lot to say about Jesus as a teacher, while John isn't as concerned with that. I could go on and on. The point is that there is a very rich and beautiful theology within each Gospel that we are missing when we harmonize the accounts.

Again, while looking into the different accounts has value as a means of examining Jesus at the historical level – like we mentioned above – we also want to acknowledge that the Gospels function at a literary level. This is where we want to pay attention to the theology of each Evangelist, tracking how they develop Jesus' story in their own unique way for the communities they cared deeply about. This is where God through His Spirit wants to meet with us since it is what He inspired and gave to the Church: four different accounts, but one testimony to the person of Jesus, and so, to the Gospel.

Reading the Gospel as Wholes
So, how do we legitimately honor this four-fold nature of the Gospels?

First, we need to begin reading the Gospels as wholes. In a lot of ways this goes back to what we discussed in our chapter on narratives. Each Gospel is its own narrative or story with its own plot, characters, and setting. Again, think of narratives as a movie. None of the Gospels is exactly alike. Matthew chooses to open his account with a genealogy (Matthew 1:1-17) and keeps reiterating that the different generations until Jesus were exactly fourteen – clearly this is important to him, but why? He then tells the story of the Virgin Birth, the visit of the Magi, and Jesus going to Egypt after escaping Herod's attempt to kill the promised king (Matthew 1:18-2:18). If you step back, some of this should be familiar from other parts of the Bible, namely, the story of God sending Israel to Egypt through Joseph, and the story of God saving Moses from being murdered by a vicious king who similarly killed children (Exodus 1:15-22; 2:1-8).

So, what is Matthew doing here? Clearly it is deliberate. Well, this introduces a very important theological point for Matthew: just as Israel was considered God's son throughout the Old Testament (Exodus 4:22-23; Hosea 11:1), so Jesus is also uniquely God's Son (Matthew 2:15). Even more so, Jesus is uniquely identified with Israel: the original prophecy of Isaiah, which referred to his son Maher-Shalal-Has-Baz conceived through his prophetess wife, and who embodied the remnant God planned to save from Assyrian destruction (Isaiah 7-8), is applied to Jesus. Within Isaiah God made it clear that the child was an omen that portended Israel's coming doom and redemption, and the same is now true of Jesus. Through him God will both judge and redeem the nation (Matthew 21:33-45). In this role, Jesus is the embodiment of Israel who relives their history: as they went down into Egypt, so does Jesus. As they were saved from an angry king's intent to annihilate them, so was Jesus. Both Israel and Jesus, as God's son/Son "were called out of Egypt" (Hosea 11:1; Matthew 2:15).

Luke, Mark, and John do something very different, but you get the point. They each are creating different settings, plots, and characters to paint a very unique picture of Jesus and the purpose of his mission. When their accounts differ, that is normally a clue into the Evangelist *choosing* those differences to create their own account. In this sense, you want to treat it very much like a narrative. Resist the desire to harmonize and pay attention *to the differences.* Those differences will often help illuminate their unique interpretation.

Second, as a story it follows the same rules as narratives. Let's reiterate these again. Storytellers give clues by repeating things. You may hear a key phrase or sentence get repeated. You may have images that keep re-appearing. Earlier, we used Star Wars as a reference: the idea of the Force, the idea of faith in adversity, the idea of a small band of rebels defeating a great, evil Empire. All of these ideas tell us that the storyteller wants us to go away and think about the use and misuse of power, what it means for something to be unified, and how change happens. It isn't through aggression, but through patient struggle, and that even the "little guy" can turn out to be an all-powerful Jedi. Within the Gospels, these repeated ideas can be numerous. Let me illustrate this from John's Gospel and how several of his themes come together in his portrayal of the crucifixion.

John has a unique portrayal of Jesus. Beginning with his prologue (1:1-18) he describes Jesus as the preexistent Word who was with the Father. This preexistent Word became flesh and lived among us (1:14). As part of this portrayal, John describes Jesus' mission as being a pattern where he first comes down from heaven (John 3:13; 6:33, 58), only to return their again later (6:61). To underscore this he organizes his account around this theme.

First, he has the prologue (1:1-18) that lays out his portrayal, then the rest of chapter 1-4 lays the foundation of the calling of the disciples followed by two significant events. These events lay out John's perspective on what Jesus' mission is all about. First there is the changing of water to wine (2:1-12) and then the cleansing of the temple (2:13-25). These two events correspond to two discourses that explain what they mean. The changing of water to wine is explained in the conversation with Nicodemaus (3:1-36), and the conversation with the woman at the well explains the cleansing of the temple (4:1-54). Both have to do with Jesus' transformation of Jewish customs: ceremonial washings and the temple.

Chapters 5-12 is the heart of the ministry. Here, Jesus explains how he has come down from heaven to bring life and will soon return to heaven. Chapters 13-17 contain a "farewell discourse." Jesus explains that he will soon be leaving to go back to the Father, but will return again soon. In the interterm he will send the Helper/Spirit to help us understand what he meant by what he taught us and to help us learn things he wanted to tell us, but that we were not yet ready to hear.

As part of this down/back up pattern John understands Jesus crucifixion as the beginning of his return journey. John therefore uses a phrase to highlight this: he calls Jesus' crucifixion his "lifting up" or glorification. John means this in a literal sense as Jesus is physically "lifted up" when crucified, but also as his "lifting up" in exaltation, and in his "lifting up" to return to the Father.

John 10 is part of a larger passage (chapters 7-10) focused on the feast of tabernacles or tents. Notice that John had described Jesus as becoming flesh and "tabernacling" or "pitching his tent" among us (1:10). This hints at his having coming down from heaven. Now he will explain this more in the backdrop of the feasts of tents/tabernacles. The account begins with a conflict about Jesus' identity. The crowds are divided with the Jewish leadership discounting him. Certain Greeks however want to meet him (7:35-36).

The passage continues with more disagreements and Jesus finally healing a man of blindness. John uses blindness often to describe the human condition and our inability to see "light." The healing thus hints at spiritual awakening as well. Jewish leadership again reject the healing, and this then leads to the Good Shepherd passage. In Jewish thought a shepherd is a leader of the people. This can be a leader generally, or more specifically, a king, since a king is the ultimate leader of the nation.

Jesus then contrasts his own ministry with the Jewish leadership who had excommunicated the man healed of blindness. He characterizes them as thieves and robbers who take advantage of the people. He on the other hand loves the sheep. They know his voice and when he calls them they follow him (just as the blind man did). He then explains that he has sheep that are not included in the current sheep pen of Israel, but that when he is lifted up (i.e., returns to heaven by way of the cross) they will see him and follow him. This alludes back to the earlier Greeks who had asked to see him (7.36-38).

All of this comes to a head in John's portrayal of the crucifixion. Here, Jesus is declared the "King of the Jews" in the three known languages of the world: Greek, Aramaic, and Latin. When the Jews become angry and ask the sign to be read "he claimed to be King of the Jews" Pilate emphatically rejects it. In other words, John sees Rome as officially declaring Jesus King through its representative, Pilate. This official declaration is also written in all the known languages of the world. The Sheep from the other sheep pens can now see their shepherd (i.e., King).

Notice also that John makes it a point to mention that Barabbas was a robber. In Greek it is the same word Jesus used to describe the leadership as "robbers" in John 18.38-40. The NIV mistranslates this as "taking place in a rebellion." Ironically, then, the Jewish leaders want a robber rather than Jesus. Also ironic, "Barabbas" is Aramaic for "son of the Father." The theme of the Jewish leadership as being self-interested is therefore continued. They have chosen a robber, just like themselves, to lead the people, rather than the Good Shepherd.

To bring this together: John is an artist who has crafted his account to tell us a story. He wants us to see Jesus' crucifixion as the moment of his coronation and the moment the Shepherd calls his sheep from all nations to follow him. Those who are his sheep will see in the cross a moment of glory and will rightly begin to follow their rightful King.

This leads to our second point about how storytellers communicate their ideas. They do this by giving clues *throughout the whole story*. Again, when we walk in on a movie that is halfway through we often end up confused, and when we just watch a single scene in a movie without watching the rest we are bound to misunderstand what's important. It is exactly the same with biblical narratives. When we pick up the Bible and beginning reading Matthew in chapter five, you are essentially starting a movie that is already well underway. No wonder it can feel confusing! Again, we need to learn to read it as a whole. This means reading it from the beginning through to the end. I know sometimes that is tough with our daily time constraints, but we can read it, then come back and continue it later, all the while remembering what you were reading the day before. Learn to track the plot as it is moving. It will make much more sense.

Conclusion

The Gospel is a beautifully complex thing that has at its heart a relationship. Relationships are not the kind of thing that can be easily reduced to a set of propositions. Instead, it is often something you can only tell another person about by relating it to something else. "Well, when I am with this person it feels *like ...*"

In the same way, the Gospel Jesus brought is not easily reducible to just a set of propositions. At its heart is a human being who brings with him an entirely new *way of life.* This is why we have four different accounts that seek to capture in different language the Gospel *according to* the different Evangelists. Jesus isn't just Matthew's vision or John's or Mark's or Luke's *but all of them.* A single account doesn't do it justice and the implications of his life are so immense that it spoke to each of them and to the communities they ministered to ... and the same is true today. The Gospel he brought had unique implications for the Jewish Christians Matthew ministered to in Syria, and the Jewish and Gentile believers John ministered to in Asia Minor, and again, has something unique for the modern Christian living in the United States today or the Chinese Christian in Asia. Learn to see these different visions and you will begin to see the beautiful complexity of your Lord and your faith.

An invitation to the four Gospels is an invitation into this beautiful complexity.

CHAPTER 8

The Letters: Missionary And Pastoral Care To Churches In Need

Paul's letters are all of the following: Romans, 1 and 2 Corinthians, Galatians, Ephesians, Philippians, Colossians, 1 and 2 Thessalonians, 1 and 2 Timothy, and Titus. There are also what are known as the "General Letters," these are letters written to a general, or unknown audience by various New Testament writers. These are the following: Hebrews, James, 1 and 2 Peter, 1, 2, and 3 John, and Jude. Let's talk first about Paul's letters and then apply some of that to the General letters.

The early Christians used letters as one of the primary ways to communicate with each other. For Paul, we have to remember that he was, first and foremost, a missionary. Paul performed several "missionary journeys" throughout his life: the first from 46-49 AD, corresponds to Acts 13-14. The second was from 50-52 AD, and corresponds to Acts 15:36-18:22. The third journey was from 53-58 AD, and corresponds to Acts 18:23-21:15. Shortly afterward he was arrested and many scholars believe this is when he wrote Ephesians, Philippians, Colossians, and Philemon. Often traveling from one city to another, he would then write letters in order to deal with issues presented in the churches, coordinate future travel plans, or raise money for his "Jerusalem collection."

The General letters are often a little different. They also deal with specific issues in churches, but sometimes are written to a wider audience. Sometimes, like with the letter to the Hebrews, we do not know who wrote it or who it was written to.

One important thing to glean from all of this though is that these are real letters to *specific* people. Not general theological documents. Paul's theology in particular is what we call "task theology," which simply means it is theology in service of a specific task. Not theology, just for theology's sake. Again, Paul was a missionary and also a pastor. He, and the writers of the General letters, were trying to deal with real life issues as it was occurring to people living in the second half of the first century AD.

Let's talk a little bit then about letters.

Letters: A Conversation Between Two Parties

Perhaps the best place to start when we are looking at the letters is to recognize the obvious: they're letters. Of course, many of us don't write letters nowadays, but we are familiar with them. It is a conversation of sorts between two parties. I write a letter and send it to you. In the letter, I probably reference a conversation we may have had in the past, or I touch bases on something we want to do together in the future. You may then write me back answering some of my questions or elaborating on something I alluded to. A key point here is that letters often reference or allude to things outside of what is written on the page. It assumes a larger conversation. Also, letters are conversations between two parties. This will have immense implications for how we want to go about trying to understand Paul's letters.

Note the following passages below:

*I wrote to you in my letter not to associate with sexually immoral people— **10** not at all meaning the people of this world who are immoral, or the greedy and swindlers, or idolaters. In that case you would have to leave this world. **11** But now I am writing to you that you must not associate with anyone who claims to be a brother or sister[c] but is sexually immoral or greedy, an idolater or slanderer, a drunkard or swindler. Do not even eat with such people.* 1 Corinthians 5:9-11

Now for the matters you wrote about: "It is good for a man not to have sexual relations with a woman." 2 But since sexual immorality is occurring, each man should have sexual relations with his own wife, and each woman with her own husband. 1 Corinthians 7:1-2

In the first passage, please note that Paul references his earlier letter and the advice he had given to the Corinthian church – but this is the *first* letter to the Corinthians! How can we have a letter before the *first* letter he wrote to the Corinthians? Well, the obvious answer is that he sent an earlier letter than what we call 1 Corinthians, and that we don't have that letter anymore.

In the second passage, please note that Paul references a letter the Corinthian church *had sent to him*: "now concerning the matters you wrote about" (1 Corinthians 7:1). What follows appears to be a quotation from *their* letter: "it is good for a man not to have sexual relations with a woman" and then Paul's counter-example and pastoral advice in 7:2-6.

Again, letters are correspondences between two parties and assume a larger conversation. So, for example, when we are trying to interpret 1 Corinthians we are midway in a conversation that has already had *at least* two letters exchanged. Paul is assuming knowledge of the prior letter he wrote (that we now don't have) and he's answering questions that the Corinthians have asked him in *the letter they wrote him* (that we now don't have). Yet, there is probably even more to this: both parties have had prior interactions *in person* with each other, and both parties have had their own experiences that effect how they are responding and the types of things they are saying.

The obvious inference to all of this is that, even though letters are more straightforward forms of communication (as opposed to say, narratives) that doesn't mean they are less ambiguous. The hard truth is that when we are reading any of the letters, we are reading it with a large amount of information *missing*. Again, we are reading a letter from only one side: we only have Paul's *responses*, not the entire correspondence. In addition, the conversation probably assumes knowledge of things that we simply don't know about. We don't know who this erring Christian was whom Paul mentions in 1 Corinthians 5. What was their side of the story? What exactly was the situation of "immorality" that Paul alludes to? Not knowing the full-story means we don't know what exactly Paul is giving advice about. In 1 Corinthians 7, clearly at least some of the Corinthians believe having sex at all is sinful. This is what occasions Paul's discussion about sex in the chapter, but how does this fact influence what he says? Would he have given slightly different advice if their approach were less extreme? Finally, the letters were written two thousand years ago, in another language, and a completely different culture. When Paul discusses eating food sacrificed to idols (1 Corinthians 8-10), we don't know all the historical details of how this was done, and how it was specifically done in Corinth in the early 50's AD. We can reconstruct some of that, but we aren't completely sure.

So how do we go about reading letters?

Mirror Reading

When we look in a mirror, we see the mirror image of ourselves reflected back. We don't actually see ourselves. In the same way, when we read a letter where we only have one side of the conversation, we need to *infer* what is going on by statements in the letter we do have. We can never see the other side exactly, but we can recreate our impression of what they *probably* said. Let me explain.

If we were to sit down and read through Paul's entire first letter to the Corinthians we would be very confident in understanding a few things. First, there appears to be an issue in the church with disunity, and that disunity appears to be based in part on how people perceive different leaders. We know this because Paul explicitly tells us that in 1:10-11 that certain members of the church have informed him that they are forming small groups around the leaders they like: some like Paul, some Apollo, and others Cephas or Peter. Also, in his greeting (we will talk more about what's a greeting in a moment) he has this curious thing he adds: To the Church of God in Corinth, … with all those who in every place call upon the name of our Lord Jesus, their Lord and ours" (1 Corinthians 1:2). Why go out of his way to emphasize that the Corinthians are part of a larger community of Christians? Well, because he is setting up what he wants to discuss about unity in the Church.

Second, in his discussion about unity he appears to go on a tangential discussion about God's wisdom versus those who are "clever." This involves more than just smarts apparently. It also involves looking prestigious or well educated, and Paul makes it clear that he is not a particularly great public speaker: he spoke while trembling and not with "persuasive words" (1 Corinthians 2:3-4). He finishes this whole section discussing how the Corinthians should specifically view him and Apollos (1 Corinthians 3-4) and warns them that the Corinthians should not pride themselves on their social status, but as members of the new community God has created in Jesus (3:18-23). This gives us a clue that whatever is occurring in Corinth must involve certain people being impressed with eloquence, and Paul's contrast between him and Apollos, with Paul placing himself on the side of non-eloquence, strongly implies the Corinthians saw Apollos as particularly eloquent, and maybe even better than Paul. Or at least some in the church chose Paul, while other Apollos, and still some choosing Peter.

A few other things we can be confident about: there appears to be a running theme of sexual sin. First, in 1 Corinthians 5 and again on his advice in chapter 7, we can certainly infer that this is a potent issue occurring in Corinth. Second, the issue of disunity keeps reoccurring, except now we see that it also involves disputes on how Christians are supposed to relate to idols and food sacrificed to idols (1 Corinthians 8-11). Apparently, this is a hotly contested issue with some feeling that, since there are no such things as other gods, the idols mean nothing – why not then eat food sacrificed to nothing (1 Corinthians 8:1-6)? Paul sides with this group, but feels like there is more to be considered. The Christians who still see these idols as representing something real are offended when their Christian brothers and sisters eat that meat. Paul, therefore, urges those who think the idols are nothing to consider these Christians' feelings. In other words, love your brothers and sisters. Paul again, uses himself as an example (1 Corinthians 9). Third, there is the issue of spiritual gifts. Paul's emphasis on the greater gifts of love, again, gives us a clue as to what is going on in Corinth: some clearly think the more "showy" gifts of tongues or prophecy are more valuable, otherwise, why does Paul go out of his way to de-emphasize them?

Finally, there is an issue, with some not believing in a physical resurrection (1 Corinthians 15). This troubles Paul deeply, and leads him to explain that the resurrection is at the heart of the Gospel itself (15:1-11).

These are some basics, but hopefully you get the idea. When we read through the letters we can begin to get a sense, based on what Paul is saying, of what must be behind it. By paying close attention to the argument, the flow of the argument, and the specifics of what he says, we can make a very educated guess of what is going on.

One more helpful tip: I usually encourage my students to spend a week reading through the letter they are studying 8-10 times. Ideally, you want to sit down with the letter, let's say 1 Corinthians, and read through the entire letter in one sitting. It has to be in one sitting cause you want to get a sense of the whole letter, not just its parts. Once you are done, write down in a single sentence statement what you think the letter was about. This can be tough at first, but it will help you zero in on what is going on. The statement should be specific enough that it is clear you are talking about 1 Corinthians, and not Galatians, or something else. It should also be broad enough to encompass everything that the letter addresses. So for 1 Corinthians it should include the topics of disunity, sexual sin, food sacrificed to idols and the resurrection. Do this every time you finish reading the letter. One other thing will also begin to happen: you will begin to notice how certain sections of the letter are inter-connected. You may notice he says something in the greeting that anticipates what he elaborates on in another part of the letter. Make a note of this. Start writing things down and observe what you're seeing. As the week progresses you're one sentence statement will become more and more specific and your overall understanding of what Paul is talking about will also increase.

Structure of Letters

In our day letters follow a specific pattern: there is usually an introduction ("Dear John") followed by the body of the letter, which is where you write the content, and then a conclusion ("Sincerely, Jane).

Ancient letters also followed a specific pattern, but it is somewhat different than what we do today. Becoming familiar with this pattern will really help you get a sense of where you're at while reading it. Also, for Paul specifically, he usually does some creative things that tips his hand on what he wants to write about.

Ancient letters had the following pattern: an opening salutation, which identified the author of the letter, the letter's recipients, and some form of greeting. Then there follows a prayer or well-wishes for the reader. After this comes the body of the letter, then a final exhortation and a concluding farewell.

This is similar to our own letters, but the salutation includes both the identification of the sender and recipients, whereas we usually break this up and place the sender at the end.

Again, Paul usually elaborates on some portion of this. Typically he uses the opening (salutation and prayer) to sound off on some of the key themes he wants to address. Other times, when he is particularly upset, he may skip the opening prayer altogether, like he does when he writes the Galatians. Another thing Paul often does, is he often returns to ideas in the concluding farewell that he first mentioned in the letter's opening. We often refer to these as the "book ends" of the letter. So, for example, in Romans he first announces his travel plans in 1:8-15 and then returns to it again in 15:14-30. Understanding this means you can better interpret his ambiguous statements in 1:8-15 in light of this clearer, and more specific explanation in 15:14-30. So, again, for example, his statement in 1:13 that he has been wanting to come to Rome for a long time "to obtain some fruit among you also, even as among the other Gentiles" is explained in 15:22-29, where he says that he has been collecting money from all of his Gentile churches to give to the poor saints in Jerusalem and "when I have put my seal on this fruit of theirs, I will go on by way of you to Spain." In other words, we could be tempted to read "fruit" in 1:13 as a fruit of the Spirit, but 15:22-29 makes clear Paul is using "fruit" as a euphemism for money. He doesn't want the Roman church to feel left out since they weren't included in his "Jerusalem Collection." As he explains, he often wanted to visit them, but his missionary work has kept him from getting there yet (15:14-21, 22). Whatever slight occurred, wasn't intended!

Conclusion

The letters of Paul and the General letters is an incredibly rich repository. Unlike narratives, the letters provide an incredibly personal and rich look into the earliest churches: the challenges they faced, the love they shared for one another, and the often-contentious issues they fought over.

It also gives us an incredible insight into the passion of one of the churches most ardent missionaries, Paul the Apostle. For years I have studied these letters and been deeply moved by a man who joyfully suffered the loss of all things so that he can more deeply know his Lord (Philippians 3) and who relentlessly pursued his commission to bring the Gospel to the Gentiles. I cannot say this enough: spending time with these letters will likely change your life. Being able to see the occasional nature of the letters will show you a brilliant pastor and missionary who was able to creatively apply the Gospel to the needs of his churches, while also trying to unite a church that often had deep reservations about his Gentile churches. He is caring, easily impassioned, prone to deep discouragement, all the while moving city to city to save as many Gentiles as possible so that like a priest he can present them as a sacrifice to his Lord on the Day of Judgment (Romans 15:16). May God cause you to share this same passion by studying his life and by becoming immersed in his theology.

CHAPTER 9

The Revelation: God's Judgment On The World Order And His Commission To The Army Of The Church

Revelation is a tough book: images of dragons, the great beast coming out of the sea, the souls of the dead crying out for vindication, all of these can be very confusing. Even the letters at the beginning seem a little strange. How in the world are we supposed to relate to all this? Going to commentaries also doesn't offer help since so many commentators often come from different theological perspectives: some believe in the idea of rapture, while others don't. Some think the thousand-year reign of Jesus is a literal time on earth, while others view it as an indeterminate time that we are currently experiencing. Lots to be confused about.

Remember that our approach in this book is a little different. Writers who focus on different end-time scenarios like the millennium often approach the book from a pre-determined theological grid. They are pre-millenialist, or post-millenialist, or even a-millenialist. Our approach isn't to come at is this way, but to focus first on the genre of the book as a guide for how we should read it. Building from genre, we then want to *let the book speak for itself* by defining it own terms (biblical theology). Whenever those terms are ambiguous, we would rather live with the ambiguity than seek to define it – or at least acknowledge that there is ambiguity and our interpretation is only one option among many viable candidates. I think if you take this approach, you will feel much better.

Also, remember what I mentioned in the first chapter: as you learn these interpretive skills you will begin to develop confidence. Sometimes agreeing, sometimes disagreeing with others around you. This is okay. Again, you are made in God's image and likeness and he believes that you are capable to understand His Word. As you begin to develop your own understanding of Revelation you can then begin to see which end-time approach seems to fit best with the text (a small hint: I don't think any of them really capture it! They all have strengths and weaknesses). Some may resonate and others may not, but regardless, you will now have an informed opinion. This is what is most important.

The Revelation: Three Genres in One Book

The first thing to note about Revelation is that it isn't simply one genre, *but three.* This alone is partly what makes it so complex. Let's look briefly at each one.

The Revelation as a Letter

Perhaps the easiest genre to begin with is the genre of letter. Revelation is framed within this genre and shares all of its basic features. Note, for example, the beginning of book (Revelation 1:4-7):

4 John,
To the seven churches in the province of Asia:
Grace and peace to you from him who is, and who was, and who is to come, and from the seven spirits before his throne, 5 and from Jesus Christ, who is the faithful witness, the firstborn from the dead, and the ruler of the kings of the earth.
To him who loves us and has freed us from our sins by his blood, 6 and has made us to be a kingdom and priests to serve his God and Father—to him be glory and power for ever and ever! Amen.
7
"Look, he is coming with the clouds,"
*   and "every eye will see him,*
even those who pierced him";
*   and all peoples on earth "will mourn because of him."*
So shall it be! Amen.

*8 "I am the Alpha and the Omega," says the Lord
God, "who is, and who was, and who is to come, the
Almighty."*

And the end of the book (22:17)

*21 The grace of the Lord Jesus be with God's people.
Amen.*

In addition, John addresses his hearers in the first
person (I … you …). The fact that the Revelation is a
letter means that, similar to Paul's letters, Revelation
is very context specific. In other words, this isn't
simply a general revelation, but also a message that
had special relevance to the seven churches in Asia
Minor. We need, therefore, to be sure we take the
historical context of these churches to heart as we
seek to understand it.

The Revelation as Prophecy

The Revelation is not simply a letter, however, but a
prophetic word to the seven churches. Remember
what we learned about the prophets, though, in our
earlier chapter on them: to prophesy doesn't just
mean to *foretell* the future, but to *forth-tell* God's word
to His people. The prophets are covenant enforcers
and spoke-persons for God. Similarly, just as the Old
Testament prophets were covenant enforcers who
sought to bring Israel back to covenant loyalty, so
here, John seeks to call the Church back to loyalty to
its own covenant with God through Jesus.

Note the way John himself describes what he has written in 22:18-19:

18 I warn everyone who hears the words of the prophecy of this scroll: If anyone adds anything to them, God will add to that person the plagues described in this scroll. 19 And if anyone takes words away from this scroll of prophecy, God will take away from that person any share in the tree of life and in the Holy City, which are described in this scroll.

Two times John refers to his writing as a "word of prophecy" (22:18, 19, see also 1:3). Similarly, the "testimony of Jesus" for which the churches are suffering (1:9; 20:4), is "the spirit of prophesy" (19:10). Finally, the God who inspired John's message is "The Lord, the God who inspires the prophets" (22:6) and it is by this Spirit that John received it (1:10-11).

This prophetic tone is seen again and again throughout the book. Within the seven letters, Jesus is either exhorting the churches to continue on in their good behavior (Revelation 2:8-11, 12-13, 18-19, 24-28; 3:4-6, 7-12) or warning them of their bad behavior (Revelation 2:1-7, 14-16, 20-23; 3:1-3, 14-21). In fact the final message of the book is one long extended prophetic word (22:10-21):

10 Then he told me, "Do not seal up the words of the prophecy of this scroll, because the time is near. 11 Let the one who does wrong continue to do wrong; let the vile person continue to be vile; let the one who does right continue to do right; and let the holy person continue to be holy."

12 "Look, I am coming soon! My reward is with me, and I will give to each person according to what they have done. 13 I am the Alpha and the Omega, the First and the Last, the Beginning and the End.

14 "Blessed are those who wash their robes, that they may have the right to the tree of life and may go through the gates into the city. 15 Outside are the dogs, those who practice magic arts, the sexually immoral, the murderers, the idolaters and everyone who loves and practices falsehood.

*16 "I, Jesus, have sent my angel to give you[a] this testimony for the churches. I am the Root and the Offspring of David, and the bright Morning Star."
17 The Spirit and the bride say, "Come!" And let the one who hears say, "Come!" Let the one who is thirsty come; and let the one who wishes take the free gift of the water of life.*

18 I warn everyone who hears the words of the prophecy of this scroll: If anyone adds anything to them, God will add to that person the plagues described in this scroll. 19 And if anyone takes words away from this scroll of prophecy, God will take away from that person any share in the tree of life and in the Holy City, which are described in this scroll.

20 He who testifies to these things says, "Yes, I am coming soon."
Amen. Come, Lord Jesus.

Finally, throughout the book, John mentions the prior saints who have maintained their witness, even to the point of death (Revelation 6:10; 19:2). Jesus is even portrayed as the One who has similarly testified to the point of death and overcome (1:5, 18; 2:8; 3:7, 14; 5:1-10; 12:5-6; 17:14-18). In this sense, Jesus is the ultimate example for us of covenant loyalty to the point of death itself. He has overcome precisely as the lamb who allowed himself to be killed.

The Revelation as an Apocalypse
Perhaps the most difficult aspect to Revelation is that it is an apocalypse. This is tough because we do not have anything really akin to this in our own culture. Within the ancient world, however, these types of books were fairly familiar. They originated in the visions of Daniel, Ezekiel, Zechariah, and parts of Isaiah and shared some of the following characteristics:

First, they are often concerned with a coming judgment and salvation, but rather than being concerned with God's act within the prophet's own time, apocalyptic literature envisioned a cataclysmic judgment breaking into history at the end of the world. Part of this is because apocalyptic literature tended to be written during times of great persecution or oppression.

Second, apocalyptic literature tended to communicate their ideas through bold images. John is told to write down what he "sees" (1:19). These images are found within visions based on fantastic and non-literal ideas: dragons, a beast with seven heads and ten horns, a woman clothed with the sun, locusts with scorpion tails and human heads, and so on. This is in marked contrast to the prophetic images invoked by the Old Testament prophets and Jesus. There the images are based on real life images: a mustard seed, a vine, an unfaithful marriage.

Third, there is a fondness for symbolism in numbers. Note throughout the Revelation how many times the number seven is mentioned, for example.

One final note on this topic: the very name of the book, the Revelation, is essentially an apocalyptic idea. Except here it has a uniquely *Christian* overtone. It is the "Revelation of Jesus Christ." In fact, John's claim is that this is a revelation that God has revealed *to Jesus*, and Jesus has then shared that revelation with the churches through John (Revelation 1:1). Remember that throughout Jesus' earthly life he did not know the day or hour of his return (Matthew 24:36; Mark 13:32). It appears that post-resurrection and post-glorification, that changed. God later did reveal to Jesus more about this coming end and he later shared it with his Church. That is essentially what this book is really all about.

Conclusion

The Revelation is really three genres uniquely combined into one. This is what makes it so challenging. These three genres have some important implications for how we need to read it.

First, as a letter, Revelation is *context-specific.* These end-time visions are not simply about a distant future, but have immediate implications for the churches spread throughout Asia Minor. This means some of the images are no doubt alluding to *historical events* at the time. They may mean more than just that, but certainly not less than that.

Second, as prophesy, the Revelation is calling us to action. The Revelation is not about learning the end-times so we can have nice charts or have an increased awareness into the secret workings of God on CNN, but is instead about summoning you to covenant loyalty. This loyalty may mean having to die for your faith – that's why Jesus is so often mentioned as the faithful witness who died and rose again, and why the saints are also the martyrs. Likewise, as prophesy, the message is not simply about the end of the world, but about the conflict between good and evil *going on right now.*

You see, the Christians John is writing to were undergoing immense hardship. They were being threatened with persecution, and even martyrdom, but were also being tempted to compromise their faith. Whether through food sacrificed to idols or the temptation to give in to the Roman state, which worshipped the Emperor, they had to remain loyal. The same is true today. Daily you are being threatened with a temptation to compromise your witness: don't! Jesus wants to you follow his example and remain pure (22:14-15).

Finally, as an Apocalypse, Revelation is highly symbolic. It communicates its ideas through fantastical images like we described above and promises a cataclysmic upheaval at the end of the age.

All of these combined are what make Revelation so challenging, but also so rewarding. In fact, Revelation is the only book that promises a blessing for those who will study it (Revelation 1:3; 22:17)! While the Bible as a whole promises blessing, Revelation distinctly says that its message will reward those who devote themselves to learn it. That is a pretty significant divine endorsement!

CONCLUSION

The Bible is an incredible book, but also a challenging one. My goal has been to give you some basic tools so you can begin to build confidence in reading and interpreting it.

I mentioned in the first chapter that there are three important tools: a good translation, biblical theology, and genres. This book has focused on genres, while future books in the Bible Notes series will build on this to help you learn the biblical theology of each book in the Bible. These future books will combine some of what we have discussed here since I cannot be sure someone will take the time to read this book first or may simply just want to dive into a specific biblical account. Those smaller books will therefore not assume this book has been read.

Regardless, though, I hope you have found some of these basic concepts on genres to be helpful. I also hope you will take a look at our other books to help you begin to get your bearings on how different writers think and talk about God and His plan for the World.

Remember: you are made in His image and likeness. You are more than capable to learn God's Word and I think that as you do so, you will find it absolutely comes alive. God's Word has been a continuing adventure and joy in my life, but it really became that when I learned how to really understand what I was reading. I truly hope the same for you! God Himself counsels you to do so, and promises that you will find rejuvenation and stability in your life once you do:

Blessed is the man who does not walk
in the counsel of the wicked,
Nor stand in the way of sinners,
nor sit in company with scoffers.
2
Rather, the law of the Lord is his joy;
and on his law he meditates day and night.
3
He is like a tree
planted near streams of water,
that yields its fruit in season;
Its leaves never wither;
whatever he does prospers.

Psalms 1:1-3

SUGGESTED READING

There are several great books on how to read and interpret the Bible that deals with its various genres and sub-genres. Are book has been deliberately brief, but if you would like further resources here are some below that I've found really helpful:

BEGINNING

Stuart, Douglas and Fee, Gordon. *How To Read The Bible For All Its Worth,* Grand Rapids: Zondervan, 1993.

Russell, Walt. *Playing With Fire,* Grand Rapids: NavPress, 2000.

INTERMEDIATE

Klein, William, Blomberg, Craig, L., and Hubbrad, Robert. *Biblical Interpretation,* Dallas: Word Publishing, 1993.

SKILLED

Alter, R. *The Art Of Biblical Narrative*, New York: Basic Books, 1981, and *The Art Of Biblical Poetry,* New York: Basic Books, 1985.

Bar Efrat, S. *Narrative Art In The Bible,* Sheffield: Almond, 1989.

Made in the USA
San Bernardino, CA
29 November 2017